ACTIVITIES & IDEAS TO ENRICH YOUNG CHILDREN'S LANGUAGE

ALSO BY DONNA CASTLE RICHARDSON, ED.D.

Reading with Children Book Series

This book is an important addition to the Reading with Children Book Series and is designed for parents, grandparents, and early childhood educators as a guide for use with young children as they learn about the world around them and learn to enjoy books based on research and best practices in reading.

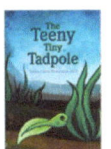   

Reading with Children Book Series:
The Teeny Tiny Tadpole
Little Lilly Ladybug
Birds Being Birds
Parenting Handbook: Teaching Your Child to Read Naturally

Activities & Ideas to Enrich Young Children's Language

A parenting handbook

DONNA CASTLE RICHARDSON, ED.D.

Illustrated by Lindsy Neely

Educational Dynamics, LLC.

Published by Educational Dynamics, LLC

Copyright © 2021 by Donna Richardson, all rights reserved
Watercolor artwork by Lindsy Neely

All rights reserved. No part of this book may be reproduced or transmitted in any form whatsoever without written permission from the publisher except in the case of brief quotations embodied in critical articles and reviews.

First Printing, 2021

Library of Congress Cataloging-in-Publication Data is available

ISBN 978-0-9987753-9-5 (paperback)
ISBN 978-0-9987753-8-8 (ebook)

CONTENTS

Also by Donna Castle Richardson, Ed.D.   iii
Dedication   ix
Introduction   xi

PART I - LANGUAGE, VOCABULARY, AND READING DEVELOPMENT

1	Building Language During Daily Experiences & Conversation	2
2	Providing Rich Vocabulary Building Experiences	7
3	Reading Together for Future Reading Success	16

PART II - SOCIAL LEARNING & EMOTIONAL DEVELOPMENT

4	Social Learning	23
5	Emotional Development	30

PART III - SCIENCE, MATHEMATICS, & TECHNOLOGY

6	Science	42
7	Mathematics	47
8	Technology	56

PART IV - CREATIVE ARTS

9	Art	65
10	Music	70
11	Drama	74

Summary   77
Resources & References   79
About The Author   88

This book is dedicated to my wonderful father, Dr. A.D. Castle, who was my model for how to live my life. He was one of the kindest and gentlest individuals. Most important, he taught me that everyone is unique and to respect others. This book is an inspiration from a book, Practical Ideas and Activities for Preschool Enrichment Programs, he wrote in 1966 for early childhood programs such as Head Start when it first started. The book was a timely resource for a new federal program targeting the early education of preschool disadvantaged children. In a dream, Daddy told me to rewrite his book for parents and update it. This book has been a labor of love, and I hope it can be used by parents and early childhood educators to enrich many children's lives. The content includes historical and current research with the major focus on ideas and activities for best practices to enhance young children's vocabulary and expand their experiences. I want to thank my editor Colleen Baines and my illustrator Lindsy Neely and Janelle Neely for their guidance and contribution. I especially want to thank, Christy Richardson, my daughter-in-law, for the time she took to read and format the text. I want to thank my friends and family who provided positive feedback about the content of the book.

INTRODUCTION

Today, as never before, children enter a world of competition with access to knowledge at their fingertips. Developing knowledge and understanding of the world is centered in the home and preschool during the early years. Early experiences need to promote intellectual, social, emotional, and physical growth in a safe, healthy, and nurturing environment to provide the framework for children's future success.

Activities and Ideas to Enrich Young Children's Language focuses on informing parents and early childhood educators on how to create a stimulating learning environment for children during the early years to enrich language and vocabulary. This is the fifth book in the Reading with Children Series. The companion book, *Teaching Your Child to Read Naturally: Parenting Handbook,* is designed to assist adults in how to read using interactive reading techniques to teach young children reading strategies. Three of the author's children's books, *The Teeny Tiny Tadpole, Little Lilly Ladybug,* and *Birds* Being Birds, are designed to link and use the information from the two adult parenting books with children.

This book is designed to focus on enrichment for young children and is filled with ideas for activities parents and educators can use to expand early learning experiences. Preschoolers are naturally curious about the world and enjoy exploring and experimenting. This book is a resource full of ideas for creating a stimulating learning environment for children.

Young children readily become captivated with the technology available to them. Parents and teachers must accept the challenge to interact and communicate with young children rather than provide constant escape into a variety of electronic gadgets. Electronics are a special avenue for learning, but real hands-on experiences provide a balance for understanding and knowledge.

Our future is at-risk. Children must learn to communicate with others and develop caring attitudes and dispositions. They need to interact with family members, other children, and adults in authentic ways. Going beyond everyday life experiences in the home or preschool can be a stimulus for learning and promoting critical thinking and problem solving.

The information and activities in this book can be used to provide parents with ideas to stimulate children's natural curiosity and interests. In the book, *How the Brain Learns to Read*, David Sousa identifies building children's vocabulary as the most important literacy intervention parents can make. The activities in this book provide suggestions for building knowledge and vocabulary. The home and school should be set up to stimulate learning using a variety of early childhood materials from crayons, educational toys, computers, special events, museums, businesses, and excursions. Also, suggestions and ideas for activities and events to do with children are included as prompts for parents, grandparents, and early childhood educators.

This book is divided into four sections. The practical ideas and activities suggest prompts to optimize the expansion for planning daily experiences and special adventures for young children to expand children's knowledge and skills so they can enter school ready to be successful learners.

- *Part I - Language, Vocabulary, & Reading Development*
- *Part II - Social Learning & Emotional Development*
- *Part III - Science, Mathematics, & Technology*
- *Part IV - Creative Arts*

The first section suggests activities to expand knowledge, language, and reading development. The second section provides enrichment ideas for social learning and emotional development. The third section focuses on ideas for teaching science, mathematics, and technology. The final section includes creative activities for art, music, and drama. These sections are recommended from *Practical Ideas and Activities for Preschool Enrichment Programs* (Castle and Porter).

An early childhood filled with rich experiences can stimulate and motivate children to be lifelong learners. Young children are naturally curious. Adults bear the responsibility for creating the environment in the home, at school, and during community activities designed for young children. **"TEACHABLE MOMENTS"** occur when the child is ready to learn new information and the adult responds at that moment.

Parents should be alert for teachable moments that present themselves during normal daily life. The adults in children's lives are essential to creating the environment that fosters later interests, talents, and success (Bloom, 1985). Vocabulary growth is strongly linked with children's intellectual growth (Hart and Risley, 1-12; 1995). A strong language foundation is based on background knowledge and is essential to reading comprehension (Cunningham, 2007). Early experiences contribute to a stronger language foundation.

PART I - LANGUAGE, VOCABULARY, AND READING DEVELOPMENT

The early years are an important time for language development, which includes the growth of vocabulary and other skills necessary for reading readiness. Language development can improve reading readiness through:

- *Building Language During Daily Experiences & Conversations*
- *Providing Rich Vocabulary Building Experiences*
- *Reading Together for Future Reading Success*

Daily events provide potential first-hand experiences for learning. The daily world is a school for learning.

| 1 |

Building Language During Daily Experiences & Conversation

The early years should be a time of exploration, discovery, and experimentation to promote curiosity and interest through interactions based on many different types of experiences. Background knowledge learned during the preschool years is critical to future educational success. Background knowledge, language, vocabulary development, and academic achievement have been well documented by researchers as a crucial connection between a child's ability to read and academic achievement. The child's language foundation and vocabulary development form an essential framework for building strategies for reading and school success (Allington, 2010; Burns, Griffin, Snow, ed., 1999; Fielding, Kerr, and Rosier, 1998; Frey and Fisher, 2013; Lapp and Fisher, 2009, Marzano, 2004; Risley, 1995; Sousa, 2014).

Initially, the family home is a natural environment for children to develop, grow, and learn language. Daily experiences in the home are authentic and based on everyday situations. Family members interact and respond by talking and listening to each other, and parents need to be aware of the critical role these interactions play in the development of a child's language. There are also unlimited opportunities within the community for providing rich experiences for expanding children's language skills.

Many children today experience childcare or preschool during the early years. These environments should be selected with consideration for whether they will provide opportunities to build concepts and expand a child's knowledge in a way that ensures readiness for school. Parents should inquire about the curriculum and evaluate prospective early childhood programs based on whether that curriculum provides rich learning experiences to enhance a child's language skills.

As adults interact with children, they should provide many exciting moments to help children develop language. Adults can model the use of language by carefully explaining what is happening during the daily experiences for children. Eating a meal together is a simple opportunity to talk not only about food, current events in the news, family stories, special past or future family trips, and plans. Parents can demonstrate interest in what children have done during the day and encourage them to talk about their activities. Children love to hear adults tell stories about what they have done. Life becomes more meaningful as they share their experiences.

Vocabulary development takes place in meaningful contexts with adults, siblings, other family members, and guests. A child's experiences can be highlighted by an adult describing what is happening such as, "Tommy is eating a triple-decker chocolate and strawberry ice cream cone."

Experiences beyond the home provide chances for adults to extend and enrich a child's language. The local community is full of rich opportunities for family excursions. Talking with the child about what is being seen and experienced will build strong memories and enhance understanding. Oral descriptions and interactions that include asking questions and encouraging children to talk about what they are seeing and doing helps children remember events and adds meaning to the experience.

Grandparents or other family members can help by providing trips and visits to special places. Shopping at stores, going on trips, visiting parks, attending ball games, and other special activities like nature walks are filled with adventures. A simple walk in the park can provide an opportunity to promote the development of oral language. Naming objects in the environment provides a basic language model. Pointing out trees and flowers and identifying and discussing similarities and differences, with the child participating, is an essential skill to develop readiness for learning to read when the child is somewhat older.

Entertaining children with games while traveling, whether for a short or long period in the car or by some other means, is another opportunity for encouraging language. A simple game can be played by each child taking a color of car and counting which color appears on the road most frequently. When the toddler begins to ask, "What's that?" a new world begins to open, and the child begins to realize that everything has a name. By providing a label, such as "That is a big red sports car," adults respond to a child's curiosity. This type of interaction also has the added advantage of making the child feel valued.

Another way to support children's vocabulary development is by repeating what they say then adding words to expand their sentences. The child may say, "Red car." The parent can expand upon the language and say, "The car is a big red Ford." This is a natural way to teach and build language during family events and interactions.

Talking and listening to children is crucial. Through such interactions, children learn not only about the verbal aspects of language, but also about other elements of communication such as body language and turn-taking in speaking. From others, children learn about appropriate eye contact, facing a speaker, and listening to others. They learn how the flow of interchange works and gradually begin adding to conversations more often.

> Tell the child about funny and cute things he or she has done during the day or in the past. Children love to hear stories about what they did from an adult perspective. A bedtime experience can be very special when the story is about the child.

During the early years, providing labels for objects is important. People, often family members, pets, places, toys, food, and other everyday objects provide the stimulus for learning the first words. The thrill of the child making first sounds that are associated with family names such as "Mama" and "Da Da" motivates parents to reinforce the child's use of words. Most parents follow the pattern of teaching their children to say "bye-bye". Learning the names of body parts is also a natural step in building language. Children's early language often progresses in a predictable way, from learning names for family members, favorite foods, and body parts such as eyes, nose, ears, and mouth then label of things in the environment. Basic words are learned early as children hear adults speaking.

Hearing language models is one of the most important ways that children learn. Talk to the child about objects during daily experiences. For example, conversation can surround fruits, vegetables, cereal, drinks, and other foods that the child is eating during a snack or meal. Simple toddler picture books can provide prompts for language building. Encourage the child to talk about the things in the environment.

One form of reinforcement for early language development is repeating what the child has said in order to clarify the meaning and validate that the child's words are important. Talking with children is extremely important to build language.

- Model language – "This is a car."
- Name new objects with descriptive language – "Look at the red football."
- Repeat what the child says – "You said, I want a glass of milk."
- Expand upon the child's vocabulary – The child says, "drink." You say, "Sammy wants a drink."
- Create a feeling of acceptance.
- Provide a variety of experiences.
- Foster interactive skills in conversation.
- Answer your child's questions.

In addition to direct interactions with the child, parent's daily conversation with each other provides a model for communicating. As parents talk, they demonstrate caring for the other person and interest about what has happened during the day and plan for future activities.

An important role of parents is to teach common courtesy. Parents are the best models for appropriate social interactions and using manners, including common expressions such as *excuse me, thank you*, and *you are welcome.*

Extend the child's language by describing the colors, shapes, and sizes of objects, numbers, and letters. Lay the foundation for children to learn to describe and categorize by describing the characteristics of toys, furniture, walls, clothing and other daily objects to them. The adult might describe a favorite toy with detail using its name and a description of its color, shape, and size. For example, when a child is playing with blocks, pointing out a particular block, the adult might say, "This block is big, blue, and square." It is also helpful for the adult to narrate what the child is doing while playing with the blocks, saying something like, "I see you are putting the blue block on top of the red block."

Simply taking time to play with your child is important. The living room, child's room, backyard, neighborhood park, and local school playground provide ideal locations for the parent and child to play together. Turning off the television can provide significant time for parent and child interaction. Routines such as eating a family meal can also be a special teaching time. Talking about the foods and the methods being used to prepare them and letting the child help with the preparation builds rapport and provides basic experiences. Including the child in the experience makes it richer for the child, in addition to creating special bonding time.

| 2 |

Providing Rich Vocabulary Building Experiences

Children love to talk about their everyday experiences. Remember to be enthusiastic about what they share to help them to feel valued. Highlight what you saw them do and encourage them to talk about their perspective. Capitalize on a child's everyday experiences to build language. Allowing children to talk freely and keeping the conversation interactive is fundamental. **Encouraging children to talk about a variety of experiences forms the foundation for language development.** Make special celebrations memorable through communication with the child about the special experience and activities.

Celebrate Daily Experiences or Special Events
- Playing a game
- Taking care of a pet
- Seeing a relative
- Taking a nature walk
- Making lunch
- Exercising, walking, yoga, sports
- Attending family picnics

- Celebrating a new sibling
- Reading a favorite book
- Planting a garden
- Playing in the park
- Dancing to music
- Reading a book
- Taking a family vacation
- Visiting a working farm
- Playing with a favorite toy
- Visiting a friend or family member
- Going to a movie
- Visiting art galleries or museums
- Singing songs
- Celebrating birthdays with family members

Shopping trips, personal care experiences, and doctor visits are ideal opportunities to talk to the child. Seeking out local community resources and events provide special activities for families. Good places to start to find these resources are local information guides on upcoming activities, which can be found in local newspapers, newsletter, local publications, tourist magazines, and on the Internet.

1. Prepare the child ahead of time for an event or activity that is going to happen by discussing where and when it will take place, what might happen, how to act, and who might be there.
2. Follow up the predictions by then talking about what is happening during the experience.
3. Later, encourage the child to recall and describe the event. After the event, the child can draw and color a picture about the event. Asking the child to describe what the picture is about can be labeled for later reading about the experience.
4. Use thoughtful questioning to encourage the child to elaborate. Using only questions to which a child can answer yes or no limits the amount of discussion that will take place. For example, in

addition to (or instead of) asking a child if she or he likes pizza the parent might say, "What do you like best on pizza? What ingredients would you need to make pizza on a flat biscuit? How long should we cook the little pizzas? Describe what the pizza tastes like."

Children love when special adults in their lives tell them about something they have done. Such interactions can form the foundation for understanding storytelling. Children also enjoy hearing stories about what they have done. Creating stories about special experiences make children feel special. Children can draw and learn to label their pictures and special experiences.

Encourage children to talk about things that are of interest to them. The statement, "The parent is the child's first teacher" comes alive in the home when parents seize teachable moments throughout the day to talk and interact with their children.

To help children build vocabulary, Marzano (2004) recommends modeling new words by saying them and describing them. As rich experiences are provided for children, they learn vocabulary, from adult models by being encouraged to say new words, describe, explain, and talk about the word. Encourage the child to describe, explain, and give an example of what the word means. After discussing the new words, have the child draw a picture or representation of what they liked. They can write what they learned about the new word, or the adult can write what the child says related his own drawing or picture representation.

The primary responsibility for creating a rich learning environment rests with parents, but grandparents and early childhood educators also provide special learning experiences for young children. Simple routines can be used to teach children, such as simply modeling and talking about how to brush teeth before bedtime stories. Children can help with chores like sorting clothes and putting them away, setting the table, and making the bed. Baskets or containers can be used to classify toys and objects that are alike and different, such as balls, building blocks, doll food, toy dishes, or small cars. These types of organizational activities can help children think and problem solve.

A Simple Language Building Breakfast Conversation

"We're going to make scrambled eggs. I need five eggs, cheese, and butter. We will use a bowl, a fork (or whisk), a skillet, and the stove. The first thing that I am going to do is break the eggs into the bowl. I am going to use the fork (or whisk) to scramble the eggs. I am turning on the burner and placing the skillet on the stove. Then, I am going to add a tablespoon of butter. Once the butter is melted, I am going to add the eggs to the skillet. Now, I am adding the cheese and stirring the ingredients together to make scrambled eggs. When the eggs get firm and consistent in texture and color, they will be ready. Other ingredients can be added for flavor."

The parent can add questions to involve the child in ownership of the breakfast preparation. Some questions to extend and expand the experience might occur naturally as the preparations for breakfast move forward.

The importance of this experience is to involve the child in the preparation. Questions can have just two choices for selecting the foods available, or they can be open ended to encourage the child to think.

"Would you like toast or biscuits? What do you think we need to get the table ready? What should we put on the table? What would be a good drink for breakfast? Would you like milk or orange juice? Do you want apple butter or grape jelly for your biscuit?"

When children have choices, within limits, they learn to make decisions.

> Playing games together should be a regular family experience. Many games are based on learning strategies, such as visual discrimination and memory, that are needed to promote essential reading skills.

Communities plan many events designed for families, educators, and children. Taking time to visit these types of events can be an incredibly special bonding experience for both child and parent. The adventure of focusing on having fun together can build wonderful memories for children. Local experiences within the community or short trips to neighboring communities and cities are easily planned. A trip to the grocery store can be the start of learning about many different foods, cooking, and family history. Foods from different countries and recipes can be explored together. Families can study themes related to their own ethnic history. Old family photos can be added to the discussion to talk about extended family members.

Visiting local businesses is a wonderful way to enrich the learning of children. Many owners will be happy to share information with children about their businesses if you make prior arrangements. Some businesses will provide tours, both informally and formally. Each business provides an opportunity to expand a child's thinking and to build memories that form useful background information.

For young children, just a ride in the shopping cart through a business can be an expanded learning experience when parents talk about what they are thinking and planning to purchase. Thinking aloud for children gives them an inside scoop on the process the adult is using to make choices.

> *Our grandson was curious after touring the Oklahoma History Museum, I gave him my iPhone so he could ask Siri complex questions about the oil industry.*

Opportunities to visit different community businesses can also be a rich and meaningful source of knowledge for children. Coffee shops are fun for children to select breakfast and hot cocoa. Focus on the business or community service as an opportunity to inform a child about different things to do and jobs people have in the community.

Sometimes family or friends who work in these organizations might be willing to make time to share information about their professions with a small group of children when prior arrangement are made. Learning about the people who help others, make lives safe, and protect people can be a worthwhile experience for children. This type of activity also teaches children to be good citizens and creates a foundation for thinking about giving to others and making the world a better place.

Planning what is going to happen before going to the doctor and dentist will help a child be prepared for the experience. Visiting police stations, libraries, government buildings, airports, and train stations are all places' children enjoy. Tourist and recreational attractions are places where beautiful memories are created. The thrill of visiting the zoo or seeing farm animals is exciting to small children. Talking about the animals and reading about them expands knowledge.

Some families make trips to tour famous ball parks and attend live ball games played at famous stadiums. Some families focus on national parks. Seeing a live circus or an ice-skating show forms an unforgettable memory for a child. Seeing historical homes, such as one belonging to a past president, or visiting a living history exhibit, like a working farm from the past, can provide an understanding of how people lived centuries ago. Understanding our national heritage and the diverse cultures we represent can enhance knowledge. Science, history, and children's museums provide unique encounters that can only be experienced in these settings. Visits to tourist and recreational attractions are essential experiences for building vocabulary and knowledge for the future.

Parades for different holidays help set the mood for special seasons of celebration. Everyone remembers their favorite holiday parade. The Fourth of July, Christmas, and Halloween are commonly celebrated in many communities, but holidays vary among different ethnic and cultural groups. Local restaurants sometimes have annual events when they share their special foods. Tasting events are always fun, especially, if they have a variety of ethnic foods. Food truck events have become more common and provide an opportunity to taste different ethnic foods. Children can experience a wealth of flavors and add language to describe colors, textures, smells, and tastes. Antique car shows, rodeos, or museum exhibits provide interest for different families. Local parks and cities will often host concerts and other events during different holidays.

The round barn is an unusual museum to visit on Route 66

Outdoor experiences are generally simple, low in cost, and offer opportunities to expand knowledge. Parents, grandparents, and early childhood educators can encourage children to observe and study animals, insects, trees, leaves, flowers, and rocks to learn new words and describe, identify similarities and differences, sort objects into categories, and make comparisons of size, shape, and color.

Nature provides a wealth of learning opportunities for children and adults to explore together. A simple walk in the park where there are ducks that can be fed is one example of a low cost, but rich learning experience. Feeding ducks and talking about their color, size, and behavior will extend the child's vocabulary. Fishing is an important experience for children. Catching the first fish provides a feeling of satisfaction. Nature walks in the woods or flower gardens can provide opportunities for exploration. Going to the local farmers market to visit a variety of booths, such as getting the face painted. The adult should provide information to support the learning experiences. All these activities help to strengthen the bond between parent and child.

These enrichment experiences provide an opportunity for children to hear and use new vocabulary which build a foundation for later reading comprehension. Just looking at flowers and talking about the type, color, characteristics, and name can be an awareness and vocabulary building experience.

The following list provides a variety of experiences to help children build language.

- **Daily routines and activities:** Playing, Preparing for bedtime, Participating in sports events, Dentist visits, Preparing meals, Putting away toys, Working in the yard, Shopping for clothes, Attending birthday parties, Brushing teeth, Planning bath time, Going to school, Going to church, Cleaning house, Eating out, Gift shopping, Selecting clothes, Taking music lessons, Going to doctor visits, Folding clothes, Grocery shopping, Attending childcare, etc.
- **Local businesses to visit:** Grocery stores, Pet shops, Theaters, Operas, Jewelry stores, Coffee shops, Bookstores, Shoe stores, Bakeries, Restaurants, Hotels, Gift shops, Clothing stores, Newspapers, Antique shops, Florists, Greenhouses, Hardware stores, Art galleries, Banks, Barber/Beauty shop, etc.
- **Community services to visit:** Police station, Post office, Schools, Library, Fire station, Court house, Hospital, Capitol building, City hall, Doctor's office, Dentist office, Airport, Bus station, Train station, Water plant, etc.
- **Recreation and tourism attractions:** Zoos, Sport parks, Circus, Museums, Amusement parks, Water park, Recreational parks, Historical sites, National parks, etc.
- **Community events:** Holiday parades, Antique car show, Fairs, Arts and crafts, Festivals, Sports events, Holiday events, Rodeos, Music concerts, Farmer's market, Food events, Church bazaars, Theater, Nature events, etc.

- **Outdoor experiences:** Local parks, Fruit farms, Flower gardens, Woodland animals, Nature parks, Vegetable farms, Meadows, Farm animals, Fishing, Woods, School playground, Mountain park trails, Ocean, River, Stream, Creek, Lake, Pond, etc.

Creating a family atmosphere for learning about new and interesting things can be fun for adult and children together. Talking about the experience can expand the children's vocabulary and enhance knowledge. Posing question about the experience and reflecting can promote comprehension and memory of special events. Following up with books, research on the Internet, and writing about the experience can foster deeper knowledge and understanding.

| 3 |

Reading Together for Future Reading Success

One of the single most important contributions that a parent can make toward a child's love for reading is simply reading books together. Supporting children as they learn to read is an important part of the reading process. Regular time set aside such as bedtime, or a special time with each child in the family can benefit relationship building within the home and school environment.

Books are essential to the early environment.

1. Select simple children's books for babies and toddlers that have one or more objects on a page. These types of books are created for toddlers and young children to learn language.
2. Talk about the pictures.
3. Then let the child name and describe the objects in the pictures.
4. This is a great language building activity.

Reading children's books daily are important for the adult to model reading so it becomes an important component of the child's life. Parents who value reading model the importance of reading.

Reading can provide a variety of opportunities to learn about the world. Books can take children to places in which they could not experience. Young children's concept and informational books can teach children about the world around them. Children acquire a vast amount of knowledge from having people read to them and help them interpret the pictures. Children can learn many concepts from pictures as they name objects.

Reading books together needs to be an **interactive thinking aloud** experience one-on-one with parent, grandparent, or early childhood educator.

> The young toddler may say, "Read book". The parent can repeat and expand upon the sentence by saying, "Heather wants me to read her favorite book, The Teeny Tiny Tadpole." This type of expanded speech provides a language model to the child from the adult.

Parents can select books that have familiar patterns and books that provide essential experiences with important literature such as folk tales. Children should have the opportunity to experience folk literature. Using books with folk tale patterns provides support for children as they learn to read. The repetition, rhythm and rhyme evolve children naturally during the reading process when folk literature and pattern books for young children are selected.

Mother Goose Nursery Rhymes, Folks Tales, and Fables

- Folk literature has historically taught the values and history within our society.
- Folk literature uses language patterns that encourage memory and interactive participation.
- Folk literature includes rhythm and rhyme.

Folk literature and pattern books provide a basic support for a young child to learn reading. When using the interactive reading cycle, children are encouraged to participate in the reading process more naturally. The technique of PRRRRing through the book should be used by parents as a format for thinking and talking aloud. More details are available in the *Parenting Handbook: Teaching Your Child to Read Naturally.*

Another way that language development occurs is through reading. Vocabulary is the foundation in which reading comprehension forms. To increase a child's vocabulary, parents model language by reading and discussing the book. Modeling the reading of books creates an environment in which children can develop a love for reading. The child also needs many different life experiences to understand what is being read.

Wordless books can be used by parents with the child to create stories from the pictures. Concept books such as the author's book, *Birds Being Birds*, teaches colors, rhymes, different settings, types of birds, music, and locomotor movements.

Environmental print, such as signs, billboards, or food items, are perfect for teaching words and letters that will have meaning for the child. Reading the symbols and recognizing letters as they relate to personal experiences enhances a child's memory. Learning to recognize restaurant signs, street signs, children's menus, toy labels, and food labels is relevant learning. Letters, colors, design, and uniqueness of the environmental print can be discussed.

> One of the most important skills in learning to read is the movement from left to right and top to bottom page progression. This can be done using your finger to point to the words on the page while reading.

Vocabulary Building with Your Child

- Build vocabulary by talking about words and what they mean in the book being read with the child.
- Create a positive feeling about books by holding the child close during the reading of the book.
- Focus on environmental print as you go places, such as restaurants by reading children's menus with the child.
- Stimulate imagination by modeling the telling of family stories and encouraging the child to create stories.
- Enhance memory by talking about the sequence of important events in stories.
- Connect personal experience in the story to similar events the child has had when relevant.
- Talk about how pictures, letters, and words have likenesses and differences.
- Encourage book knowledge to include cover, title page, beginning and ending, and author notes.
- Show the child how to look at letters and words from left to right.

Interactive reading occurs as parents talk about the story and make meaningful connections to past experiences. Motivation to read is based on enjoyment of hearing books and experiencing reading. Young children need to develop an interest and appreciation for books. Empowering children to enjoy learning and reading begins in the early years when children's curiosity is high and their eagerness for learning is open to rich experiences.

Special Reading Activity Examples

- Talk about words
- Copy words
- Talk about pictures
- Talk about letters
- Dictate stories

- Listen to stories
- Talk about sounds
- Talk about letter sounds
- Make a book
- Read Nursery Rhymes
- Remember the story
- Find missing objects
- Label picture, etc.

Cameron wrote in his book, "I had my face painted like a dog. I ate a pretzel then drank chocolate milk."

After a special experience, the child can make a book using photos from the event, dictating or telling the adult, or writing about the experience on their own possibly using a word processor if they are older. Typing the story on the computer with adult support is fun. Adding the photos to support the story make the book interesting. The child will have the memories in their book.

In summary, encourage language development by providing rich daily experiences and conversation. Reading books together builds a foundation for school success. Making books about special experiences makes reading real and meaningful. Do things together that provide teachable moments. Parents have been called the child's first teacher. Enhancing children's vocabulary through rich and meaningful experiences, helps them as they read to understand and connect with the reading materials.

PART II - SOCIAL LEARNING & EMOTIONAL DEVELOPMENT

In the fast-paced society of today, families are busy rushing to sporting events, private lessons, and other extracurricular activities. The home, community, and school are important places where children learn about social and emotional behavior. Casel (2017) lists five areas of competencies that foster social and emotional learning that should be kept in mind when interacting with children. The five areas are: self-awareness, self-management, social awareness, responsible decision making, and relationship skills. This section focuses on:

- ***Social Learning***
- ***Emotional Development***

Children initially learn how to control their behavior within the family environment and then from others as well, so it is important that they have safe, predictable home and school environments. Self-awareness begins as children learn how to express emotions and thoughts. Social awareness is learned from interacting with people, and it is the way children learn to respect the rights of others despite differences and understand how to negotiate various social norms (Casel, 2017)

Social and Emotional Areas and Suggested Activities (Casel, 2020)

- Self awareness: Use a mirror and say, "I am…"
- Self-management: Help with chores
- Social awareness: Plan kindness activities to give to others
- Relationship skills: Plan game night with family or friends
- Responsible decision-making: Write successful accomplishments to post

| 4 |

Social Learning

Children need to learn how to act and respond in different situations and are dependent upon their first social environments to learn appropriate behavior. **Adults can instill social skills by making them a regular part of daily routines and providing positive feedback with guidance as needed.** In addition to daily routines, social skills can also be taught during special occasions, social events, playing games, and family time.

Family meals provide a great opportunity for a child to learn social skills and appropriate behavior. Eating at restaurants can be a special time together when skills can also be taught without anyone preparing the meal and cleaning the kitchen. In contrast, meals at home offer the opportunity to include a child in the planning and preparation of meals as well as the clean-up after eating. This valuable interaction time allows conversation and a chance to focus on family stories, beliefs, culture, and values. Manners can be taught and modeled, whether at a restaurant or at home. Providing positive feedback to a child can increase the understanding of social and behavioral expectations. Keeping experiences positive and fun reinforces desired behaviors.

Learning manners and other social behaviors allow children to be more prepared for special occasions, such as birthdays and holidays that may take place within the context of the family or might include other people as well. Children will feel more confident if they understand table manners including eating with the mouth closed, using a fork and knife correctly, using a napkin, taking turns in conversation, and using polite words. Manners are important and can be modeled by adults and encouraged as children learn to say thank you, please, and you're welcome. Respectful behavior toward adults, such as saying, "Yes Ma'am" or "Yes Sir" can also be taught.

Children can be helped to prepare before special occasions by talking about expectations in advance or by role-playing situations they will face. This can provide children with confidence in how they should act and may help to relieve anxiety about new social situations.

Providing meaningful social learning experiences and seizing teachable moments allows adults to provide the framework that allows children to experience success in social situations. *Little Lilly Ladybug* by Donna Castle Richardson teaches courtesy and can be used to prompt the importance of manners. Children need to learn a variety of social behaviors and responses for different environments and situations to be successful socially. If they feel safe in the environment, they will feel confident about seeking guidance from adults.

How to handle and resolve conflict is a skill caring adults can teach and model during everyday situations. Children need to know how to behave in different social situations. It is important to talk about appropriate behaviors before, during, and after social situations so that children can develop social competencies.

Ideas for talking about social skills and development

- Taking turns
- Playing fair
- Sharing with others
- Respecting the rights of others
- Developing appreciation for others
- Demonstrating thoughtfulness

- Approaching others positively
- Talking about family cultural heritage
- Working cooperatively, collaborating with others
- Emphasizing family teamwork
- Negotiating solutions with others
- Resolving conflicts
- Understanding self, thinking for oneself
- Taking responsibilities for actions
- Using manners
- Developing a sense of humor
- Communicating clearly
- Asking for help
- Showing empathy
- Cleaning up, putting toys away
- Articulating needs to others
- Developing leadership abilities
- Learning self-regulation/management, demonstrating self-control
- Interacting safely, making safe choices with friends
- Talking about how to enter a group
- *(Castle and Porter, 1966; Kostelnik and others, 2002; Casel, 2017; Cox, 2019)*

Adults must respond consistently to children, especially when they have broken the rules. Encourage children to think about the event and what they think they should do rather than criticizing the child for inappropriate behavior. Ask what he or she is thinking and what actions could have been a better choice. Probe to see if they understand the expectations. Avoid criticism. Instead, respect children's thinking and discuss what is expected. Reteach, explain, and model the behavior that is expected. **Questioning rather than correcting helps both the adult and child to clarify expectations through positive communication**. Seize teachable moments to share appropriate expectations.

In cases of shared custody, all adults who play a parenting role need to keep in mind that there may be different behavioral expectations in each household. This can be confusing to children initially, and it may take some time for them to internalize the different household rules, so before criticizing children's behavior, make sure to remind them that each home has its own parental expectations. Co-parenting is more complex but respecting the child can solve many different perspectives. Some children will test limits while others will obediently follow expectations. Taking the time to directly teach expectations to children will help build their confidence.

> Our grandson loves to eat at nice restaurants with us. He learned how to eat property and to use manners and rules of etiquette. He was at a local cafe, and the waitress asked if he was finished with his food. He turned to his Pappy and said, "Can't she see my silverware is telling her that I am finished?" He learned to place his silverware diagonally on his plate from a previous trip to St. Louis while eating at a nice restaurant.

Family time provides an opportunity to model manners, taking turns, listening, and sharing. Turning off cell phones and other electronic devices during family time is important. Electronic devices take away from quality time together. Creating a caring home environment that fosters respect for others gives children an important tool for social success. Teaching values by helping children learn to identify right and wrong choices within the family helps children build character. Teaching how to follow the basic rules in society is important so that children learn to make safe choices.

Questions and statements for probing children's understanding

- What are you doing?
- What should you be doing?
- What would be a better choice?

- Show me what you should be doing.
- How can I help?

When children have consistent routines, they learn what to expect. On another note, it is important to enjoy children and family activities. Remember to compliment the child for using appropriate behavior. Adults should remember that they are guides for children. **Children learn by observing how others communicate and cooperate.** Those who learn appropriate social skills will be more successful and experience less conflict. "Childhood is, by definition, a time for learning and testing many ways of responding to social situations" (Katz and McClellan, 1997). Children need to learn that they are responsible for their own behavior and how to act around and with others in order to maintain a safe social and emotional environment.

Children need to learn about making good choices. First and foremost, choices need to keep everyone safe mentally, emotionally, and physically. Discussing good decisions is important to future success as alternative choices are discussed with caring adults. Predicting consequences of different choices with caring adults promotes problem solving and inquiry. Reflecting and remembering after social situations provides a time to think about decisions and actions.

Learning how to respond in different situations is important. One example is to talk about how expectations differ between a fast-food establishment and an upscale restaurant. Children need to understand that the appropriate behaviors, the scripts, are different. When entering a fast-food restaurant, a person generally stands in line, orders the food, pays then either picks up the food or it is delivered to the table. In a fine-dining restaurant, people wait for a host or hostess to seat them, and orders are given at the table to a waiter or waitress. Napkins, plates, and silverware are placed in a certain way generally with cloth napkins and a tablecloth. Preparing ahead of a visit to a restaurant so that children are aware of what will be expected can avoid problems out in public and helps keep the experience positive. Talking with children about how restaurants are alike and different helps them process and lays the foundation for what to expect. Time should be taken to highlight the expectations for behavior in a variety of settings and for typical daily circumstances children will encounter.

Discussing and planning helps make it more likely that the child will be successful in social situations. A trip to the grocery store can become frustrating for everyone involved if a child wants something the parent does not want them to have. Set parameters for **children** before entering the store. Explain that you are buying food for the family meals. It is an important learning experience to actively involve children in part of the shopping and decision-making by telling them in advance they will be allowed to pick a favorite cereal, fruit, vegetable, or whatever is appropriate to the shopping list. Discussing choices, you will allow the child to make before entering the store helps set expectations for behavior. Planning and communicating expectations before any experience helps build successes for children and allows their confidence in social situations to grow.

> A wise woman told me when my son was a toddler that children love pulling everything out of the toy box before playing. After they finish playing, returning everything back to the box becomes overwhelming. Children need support and help to learn simple routines.

Holding a family game night is a great way to teach children how to play, share, follow rules, negotiate, and compromise with others. Learning to win and lose is important. Setting aside a time to play together as a family is important and enhances relationships. **Children who learn to play fairly within the family unit will get along better with others outside of it** and play times with other children are likely to be more successful and rewarding. Being able to laugh and enjoy the company of others depends on a child's level of comfort in social situations. Family game time helps to build the skills necessary for successful play interactions outside the family unit. young children should be taught to share and how to play appropriately with others. Even in the same family, children vary in their social skills, perspectives, and reactions. Each day offers opportunities to talk about how to act and solve problems.

When children play with others their own age, they need to be able to test behaviors in a safe environment. Adults need to pay attention to try and observe when teachable moments occur. Playdates and interactions with neighborhood friends, participation in club, church, and sports events, time in childcare, and other community activities provide environments for learning various rules and expectations. **During social situations, children learn how to respect others, share, take turns, and communicate.** Social skills are learned within both daily and special activities by having caring adults participate in guiding and confirming behavior. Play dates with children in the neighborhood and playtime at school with classmates should be encouraged. Children need to be able to test out behavior and have supportive adults who teach, guide, and support self-regulation in safe environments.

Adult modeling of nonverbal social behaviors such as smiling, waving, making eye contact, and nodding are important. It is also important that children learn from adults that it is appropriate to take turns and listen to each other in conversations. Teaching and guiding young children through daily routines in the home or an early childhood classroom provide real life learning. **Learning occurs as expectations are made clear, routines are established, behavior is monitored, and positive guidance remains consistent.** Everyday settings provide a wealth of opportunities for teaching social skills.

| 5 |

Emotional Development

Children need a safe environment to grow emotionally. They need to experience consistent responses from adults to feel comfortable and to know how to respond. Adults should provide guidance by focusing on building the skills of communicating, cooperating, and decision making to support emotional development (Education Week Research Center on Safety and Social and Emotional Survey, 2019).

Even when children are young, **it is important to communicate, to talk with children about emotions they may be feeling and provide ways to express those feelings** (Kostelnik, 2002: 131). Providing verbal labels for emotions is one step in helping individuals learn how to express feelings and promotes self-understanding. Teaching children words such as angry, happy, or sad and asking questions such as, "Are you angry because you didn't get what you wanted?" can assist children in identifying and expressing their feelings. Adults can help children clarify feelings.

As language is developing, children have a limited vocabulary, and this frequently creates frustration because they cannot make the adult understand what they are saying. Toddlers often know what they are saying, but have difficulty clearly articulating the words to express their feelings. Adults must be patient in trying to understand what is being said.

Common Emotions & Descriptive Words to Use with Children

- **Happy** - happiness, delight, satisfaction, cheer, pleasure, joy, glad, merry
- **Anger** - frustration, annoyance, mad, disgust, boredom, fury
- **Sad** - unhappy, grief, discouraged, blue, down
- **Fear** - anxious, scared, dread, panic, fright
- **Surprise** - shock, wonder, amazement
- **Scared** - frightened, petrified, afraid, fearful, terrified

Reading books about feelings to children and discussing them together helps identify common emotions they may be trying to express. Adults need to be warm, respectful, and accepting to model emotions in a way that supports children's emotional development (Kostelnik, 2002; Casel, 2020, CSFEL).

The Center on Social and Emotional Foundations for Early Learning at Vanderbilt University recommends four steps for helping children express their emotions.

1. Explain and talk about feelings and give the emotion a name such as those listed under "Common Emotions and Descriptive Words to Use with Children" above.
2. Talk about different ways to act appropriately to express different emotions. Repeat the child's words back. Talk about ways to act based on family norms and expectations. Use pictures or books to help the child see and think about different emotions.
3. Praise the child when they talk about their feelings. Encourage the child to express their feelings. Clarify the emotion as needed by using the synonyms in the box.
4. Encourage talking about feelings and practice new ways to express feelings. When playing with the child, discuss different feelings.

Be direct and clear when providing instructions for behavior. Sending an "I message" makes expectations clear such as, "I need you to sit down". "I message's" direct children on what to do. Telling a child not to do something may get him or her to stop, but it doesn't provide them information on what they should be doing. Instead, give clear direct directions stating exactly what to do is more likely to get the preferred behavior. Provide clear directions. For example, "You don't run in the room." Instead say, "I want you to always walk while in the room to be safe." This example can add more about the why. Children need important skills of self-awareness, self-management, social awareness, relationship, decision making, problem solving, and character development (Casel, 202; Murphy, 2016, KSDE, 2013).

Self Awareness

As children develop emotionally, they need to be guided in becoming aware of their feelings and how to manage and express them in acceptable ways. This is critical to personal development. From both observation and direct instruction and practice, children learn socially acceptable ways to respond and express their emotions. It is up to adults to be aware of opportunities when social and emotional competencies can be taught and guided.

> Teaching young children about emotions can be a fun experience. Acting out facial expressions, identifying feelings of different characters in books, and playing games can be engaging ways for children to learn common words for and descriptions of emotions.

Promoting appropriate emotional behavior begins with self awareness. Children need an understanding of who they are and who they are not (Kostelnik, 2002). Self-awareness develops over time and contributes to social competence. As children learn self awareness, they need support to know who they are. The development of positive self-awareness is based on successful experiences. Adults must nurture young children so that they know who they are and feel good about themselves and what they can do.

Ask questions such as, "Did you enjoy eating at the new restaurant? What foods did you like? What foods do you not like?" or "How was school today? What did you feel was the best thing that happened? What did you learn about others? Who is your friend? What would you change about today?"

To promote self awareness, encourage children to talk about how they feel in different situations. Discuss what they are wearing for different activities. Help them learn to describe their appearance. Engage them in discussion about what they can do well, what they enjoy doing, and what they feel they need to have support to do.

Self-Management & Social Awareness

The development of self-management and social skills best occurs in environments where children have been given clear messages about what to do and what not to do. Understanding how rules and expectations are different at school from what they are at parties, visits to friend's homes, and other group settings evolves over time. Even adults are sometimes challenged in new situations. Some social skills span all social situations.

Adults can promote self-management and social skills by encouraging children the following sequence of prompts, **"What are you doing? What should you be doing? Show me."** You can add, **"Can I help? Thank you for telling me." Teach children how to act in different situations and environments.** Children need to learn about their emotions, and what is expected socially in different situations. They need to experience personal successes and be affirmed.

Point out good choices the child makes. Some prompt questions to use when children need help making a good choice are: What is a good choice now? What might be a better choice? How would that make you feel? These are types of questions that can be asked so that children learn to think about what they are doing.

Relationships

Relationships are built through thoughtfulness and kindness toward others. Listening, helping, taking turns, and sharing are important developmental steps for young children to provide them the skills needed to build relationships. Children learn a great deal from watching others, so adults need to model behaviors that provide a guide for positive ways to build relationships. Listening carefully to children and remembering what is important to them demonstrates how others work at building relationships.

Responsible Decision Making and Problem Solving

One key to successful emotional control is related to effective decision making and problem solving. Children can be taught ways to make decisions and solve problems in many situations. All parents worry about their preschooler running into the street. This is a time to talk about safe decision making, teach the importance of staying close, and hold a parent's hands when in a high traffic area. Learning to stop, look, and listen before crossing the street is an essential decision-making activity on how to be safe.

If a child is frustrated putting a puzzle together, you might provide support by asking questions such as "How does this shape fit?" or

"Where is a corner?" and "How do you know it is a corner and where do you think it might go?"

Character Development

Character development is grounded in social and emotional development. The Character Counts project at Drake University's recommends (Character Counts website) promoting six pillars of character development. First and foremost, children need to be in safe environments where they know they can be truthful. They need to know that they can make mistakes and they have support to be honest. **The six pillars provide recommendations for building character** and are briefly discussed below:

1. **Trustworthiness** – Adults need to encourage honesty and the rules for respecting others. Children need to be respected and guided safely. Self-discipline and self-regulation are learned from adults. Children need clear guidance and direction, so they know what to expect and do in different situations. They need to know when they do things correctly and how to do things in a social situation.
2. **Respect** – During their early years, children have limited experience identifying their own feelings and the feelings of others. Over time, children need to learn the golden rule of treating others in a way they would want to be treated and to respect the feelings of others. They also need to learn to respect other people's property.
3. **Responsibility** – Children need to be given small responsibilities as they are developmentally ready for them, such as taking care of their own room and helping the family in small ways so they can learn to be successful. Developing responsibility

initially involves making good choices within the limits inherent in different situations.

4. **Fairness**– Children learn to be fair by being treated fairly. They learn compassion and empathy by being loved and cared for in a safe environment. They learn to accept rules such as taking turns and sharing, in social situations. They need to know how to ask for help and how to express gratitude.

5. **Caring** – Adults need to show they care by helping children learn to finish what they start and to have a sense of satisfaction and pride in the completion of tasks. Remind children that doing their best will help avoid having to redo the same tasks. Engage children ahead of time in talking about the best way to accomplish something and then follow-through to provide encouragement and support as they undertake the task. Safe touching and complimenting children are important.

6. **Citizenship** – Children need to learn how to share, cooperate, learn to consider others, and respect the rules and guidelines in different situations and settings. Providing experience in a variety of social situations, including ways in which they can help others, helps develop citizenship.

These six principles can be used by parents to guide character development. The respect of others and self are important. Another important factor to be considered to guide children is how to treat others. Bullying is a common problem, and young children need to know how to recognize and respond to bullies as well as how to avoid bullying others. Bullying has three elements: it is the act of aggression and intended to do harm; these acts are repeated over time; and occurs within the context of power imbalance (Snow, NAEYC, 2014). Bullying is common in early childhood as children experiment and test behaviors. Talking frankly about bullying and how to treat others with respect is important.

The role of the adult is to follow-through: to guide and encourage appropriate behavior. Read books about bullying behavior and discuss them with children. According to a mega analysis on bullying by Clayton and others (2010), it suggests a bully has social and academic challenges, possesses negative attitudes and beliefs about others, has negative self-related cognition, and has trouble resolving problems with others.

Children need to be in positive home environments, early childhood classrooms, and other community situations where appropriate social skills are used. Positive social skills need to be modeled. Influences must be monitored so that appropriate intervention and redirection may take place when needed to assist children when they are faced with negative models of behavior. In this way, they learn social problem-solving skills. Children's books that focus on social skills and positive behavior play a valuable role in helping children develop social competence.

Acquisition of the vocabulary to express emotions, the development of self-awareness and self-management, and relationship, decision-making, and problem-solving skills are all critical elements in children's social and emotional development and help build character. These skills, learned in early childhood through play and interaction with others, assists children in successfully creating a positive environment for themselves and for others. Opportunities to share and get along with others, to learn to respect the rights and abilities of others, to have feelings of self-respect, personal worth, and dignity are important to children's development. Cultural heritage and unique differences need to be appreciated and honored. Through social activities, adults can provide positive guidance and support to children as they learn and grow.

PART III - SCIENCE, MATHEMATICS, & TECHNOLOGY

Adults play a critical role in encouraging young children to be interested in learning about the world around them. Learning about science and math in the home and in early childhood settings evolves from the adult's guidance. Young children are immersed in the family environment and activities parents do with them daily. Enrichment can be provided by planning activities that help children learn about science and math. Math, science, and technology activities for young children can be based on inquiry and problem solving during daily routines. Simply counting the dishes and setting the table can be a math experience of one-to-one correspondence that can add counting objects to match the family members eating.

Science, math, and technology promote the use of problem solving and thinking skills. Historically, the teaching of science and math have used the inquiry method to provide opportunities for exploration and discovery.

- *Science*
- *Mathematics*
- *Technology*

Thinking, Problem Solving, and Inquiry Skills. Science, math, and technology involve thinking, problem solving and inquiry and can be enhanced through daily routines. During playtime children can explore, discover, and invent ways of doing things. They learn during daily chores, routines, and other special experiences. Adults need to provide the language background that prepares children to understand problem solving and inquiry. Adults have the responsibility of gradually building the child's knowledge base.

As new information is being learned, it is important for adults to appreciate and respect the child's perspective. Everyday household activities offer the opportunities to help children develop the types of thinking skills they will need to approach future learning. Children can learn problem solving by determining what to do if one family member does not like tomatoes while another one loves them. Additionally, this teaches respect for likenesses and differences in others.

Remember, common household chores provide activities for children to think, problem solve, and use inquiry skills simply by placing the dishes, silverware, and glasses on the table, or putting them in and taking them out of the dishwasher. These simple activities provide an opportunity to count, classify, and organize objects. Children can learn about different parts of the dishwasher because of how it is organized. Classification and associations of different objects needed for eating and where they go in the cabinet is an everyday learning experience to encourage children to think in an organized manner.

Children can learn to categorize, organize, and sort objects through activities like setting the table or helping to sort laundry. Even helping make the family salad can be a learning experience in estimating quantities based on the number of people to be served, or adjusting ingredients based on the likes and dislikes of individual family members.

Such systematic household activities can help children learn to think, make connections, see likenesses and differences, and begin identifying relationships among objects that do and do not make sense. Sorting clothes by color and type is an easy and natural classification activity family members do regularly. Encouraging the child to help with sorting, folding, and putting clothes away after they have been washed can save the parent time. Putting clothes in dressers or chests in different drawers or areas for socks, shirts, undergarments, and pants placed by colors in different parts of lower cabinets or drawers in the dresser that a child can reach is a simple sorting or classification activity. Putting toys away in the same place can aid in organizational skills, memory and follow-through. Learning science, math, and technology can easily be incorporated into daily activities.

| 6 |

Science

Physical and biological sciences are easy to incorporate activities for young children. Biological science is the study of living things that grow and mature over time. Life cycles allow children to understand the basic theory of change as they observe how plants, animals, insects and people grow, mature, and die. Young children should be encouraged to observe their own growth. One way to do this is to provide photos that show a child's growth and change over time. Basic science associated with living things can be experienced easily in a short period of time through gardening and taking care of animals. These experiences can teach basic survival requirements. For example, plants need water, sunlight, and nourishment to survive. Animals need food, water, air, and shelter. Omit one of these and the plant or animal dies.

Physical science is another area of science that young children enjoy learning. It is the study of matter and energy and has many interesting areas, such as observing the stars and moon changes at night see patterns and talk about the universe. Finding patterns in the environment extends thinking and builds a foundation for intellectual growth and problem solving.

Cooking is a perfect way to learn about the basics of the scientific method and provides a problem-solving foundation. Drawing pictures to show the sequence of adding ingredients in a recipe before using it, organizing the ingredients, preparing the kitchen tools, mixing the ingredients, and following each of the recipe directions provide important skills in approaching problems in a step-by-step way. Using measuring cups and spoons helps children begin to understand the relationship between numbers and measuring. Baking a cake can show how liquid can become a solid. Basic physical science activities can be used with children to discover, explore and invent ideas.

Young children learn science through active involvement by exploration, discovery, and creative thinking. Learning facts can be fun through the different science activities suggested. Young children are naturally motivated to learn from observations as they ask questions and clarify understanding. Weather is another subject children can learn first-hand by observing wind, rain, clouds, rainbows, snow, hail, and sleet.

A field trip at a local nature and science museum

Children learn through hands-on experiences (Wilson, 2019). In the home and in early childhood environments children need to be able to explore and play. Home and early childhood classrooms environments can be designed so children can discover and construct their own wonderful ideas (Wilson, 2019). They should be encouraged to explore, discover, ask questions, and make guesses about the world and how it operates, and draw conclusions.

Set up an environment that allows children to problem solve by classifying objects. As children develop observation skills, they can make collections of many objects in the environment such as rocks, shells, seed pods, and pine cones. Probing questions help children justify their decisions and develop language skills. **Using open ended** questions that have more than one answer, can foster young children's scientific thinking.** Appreciating how children think is especially important.

The child's room, home play area, backyard, classroom, and preschool playground can be set up to inspire inquiry and creative thinking skills. Divide the room into different areas. Use baskets for classifying toys on shelves in the play area by types such as cars, toy food, puzzles, shapes, blocks, balls, and other similar objects. After children pull out objects, help guide them in returning items to a consistent place. Children sometimes get overwhelmed and need help to put toys away using organizational skills.

With the right type of materials children can explore and discover how things work. An old log with nails and a hammer can be fun items for children. An old table with tubs can be used for sand or water exploration. A recipe for bubbles can be found on the Internet. Using bubbles is a fun activity that can be used to observe how the wind moves things around, how some things are lighter than air, and how blowing just the right way, not too hard or too soft, is necessary to create bubbles.

The following lists provide a variety of science related activities and ideas to incorporate into learning with children.

Basic Science Topics & Simple Activities

Physical Science
- **Cooking** - Help with mixing ingredients for baking
- **Stars, meteors, constellations** - Lay on the ground and study the stars
- **Moon, sun, sky, universe** - Draw the moon shape over a month
- **Planets, space** - Read a book about the planets and solar system
- **Weather** (rainbows, rain, clouds) - Make an art project of the different clouds (blue paper, cotton balls, glue)

ACTIVITIES & IDEAS TO ENRICH YOUNG CHILDREN'S LANGUAGE - 45

- **Tools, machines** - Provide a child's woodworking table
- **Forms of water** - Setup a bubble table with wands
- **Bodies of water** (creek, river, sea) - Discuss bodies of water
- **Rocks** - Identify and classify different rock types
- **Ocean, seashell, starfish** - Compare different seashells
- **Temperature** - Chart daily changes in outdoor thermometer

Biological Science

- **Trees, grass, flowers** - Draw the plants outside or look at them under a microscope
- **Seeds, plant growth** - Plant a flower or vegetable garden
- **Types of food** - Classify the food at dinner
- **Zoo animals** - Visit the local Zoo
- **Farm animal** - Field trip to a child friendly farm
- **Life cycles** - Classify baby and adult animal pictures
- **Care of pets** - Chart feeding and watering family pets
- **Insects** - Explore the yard for insects
- **Birds** - Use binoculars to look for birds
- **Tadpoles and frogs** - Study types of frogs on the Internet
- **Baby animals** - Match baby animals to adult animals
- **Human body** - Measure growth and weight over time
- **Skeletons** - Look at different animal skeleton parts
- **Bacteria** - Compare clean hands and dirty hands

Basic Scientific Big Ideas & Concepts with Activities

- **Systems** (life cycle needs to live) - Study family photos
- **Models** (human body) - Find an example of the digestive system on the Internet (other systems)
- **Change** (plants) - Draw the changes in a plant

- **Cause and effect** (weather) - Listen to weather forecast
- **Scales** (weight, size, and quantity) - Track weight and height
- **Patterns** (colors, size, texture, shape) - Explore patterns in toys

Thinking & Inquiry Skills to Foster Scientific Thinking

- **Classification** (sorting things that are alike and different based on criteria)
- **Associations** (seeing and determining relationships based on a common characteristic of how things go together)
- **Patterns** (looking for common characteristics and sequencing that repeat)

Materials & Toys for Scientific Exploration

- Bucket, digging and measuring tools
- Hammer, screwdrivers and nails
- Soil, cups, pitchers, and seeds
- Magnets
- Large and small bubble wands
- Magnifying glasses
- Old machines without plugs
- Pulleys, inclined planes, and ramps
- Insect nets and cages
- Thermometers, etc.

Science can be taught using everyday objects and through daily activities and experiences. Watch for teachable moments and be aware of the basic concepts' children need to know. Promote scientific thinking through activities that give children practice classifying, organizing, and problem solving. Allow them to explore, discover, and form new ideas and concepts.

| 7 |

Mathematics

Early childhood concepts of counting, identifying numbers and shapes, telling time, counting money, and understanding fractions and measurement form the foundation for learning math. Young children need to be able to explore and learn the vocabulary of math to be successful in school. This section will suggest ideas and activities for exploring math.

There are many ways to learn math and children's books about numbers are widely available. Introducing numbers through books can be followed with counting activities using small toys, counting blocks, or other appropriate objects. Learning to identify opposites and directional words can give young children an advantage when they enter school. Children's books are one way to teach the concept of opposites and the importance of likenesses and differences that form the foundation for critical thinking in math. Turn the lights on and off, night is dark, and day is light are based on simple everyday experiences.

Teaching directional words can also help children be more successful when they begin school. Words and phrases like *under, besides, on, next to,* and *inside o*f can be taught using simple directions that require children to put a ball or some other object on, under, besides, next to, or inside of a shelf, box, cabinet, or some other object. Directional words are essential for students to follow later directions in completing school assignments.

> **Directional Words:**
> on, under, over, up, above, down, around, in front of, behind, inside, between, left, right, middle, outside, below, first, last, out, in, near, far, here, there

Talking with children about where things go and having them participate in straightening up their toys provides them not only with an opportunity to learn responsibility but offers the perfect chance to practice directions.

Part of mathematical knowledge is learning how numbers are used in everyday life. Math in the home can occur naturally as children think about situations in everyday life such as having two cookies and giving one to a sibling and understanding that they will then have only one left.

Activities to Help with Big Ideas in Math

- **Patterns** - Looking for patterns that repeat and making bead patterns by stringing them on shoelaces can be a perfect start
- **Order** - Putting number shapes in order helps build numeral awareness and recognition
- **Compare** - Adding sets of objects to each numeral above can help children compare the number of objects to the numerals
- **Sequence** - Putting the numerals and number of objects in a line sequence from left to right and top to bottom can be a simple reading readiness and mathematical experience
- **Fractions** - Eating fractions of the pie, such as 1/4, 1/6, or 1/8 of the pizza, or pie, can be a tasty experience
- **Parts to whole** - Talking about how the pizza or pie are a whole until we cut them into fractions

All the examples for learning big ideas in math can be transferred from daily experiences into school activities. It is important to watch for situations so that meaningful learning can occur.

Basic Mathematical Thinking

- **Classification** - Sorting things that are alike and different based on
- **Associations** - Seeing relationships of how things go together
- **Patterns** - Looking common characteristics and sequences that repeat

Adults need to develop an awareness of opportunities to teach math. When children are provided with chances to count objects, they increase their number knowledge and awareness. Measurement can be learned by measuring food and other objects. Talking about time for daily activities by looking at the hands on the clock or the digital time can help children learn about connections to time and daily routines. Shapes are everywhere! Once children learn the names and characteristics of basic shapes, they can identify them in daily experiences. Providing a toy cash register can help the child learn about the world around them and begin to develop the concept of what money is and does. Separating fruit such as an orange into segments can be an exercise in learning parts of a whole and halves, which is the beginning of the study of fractions. Children enjoy learning to read a thermometer and what the degree symbol looks like.

Hands-on cooking activity with my grand-daughter Brianna

Counting - *Once children learn to count by rote, then move to **counting objects** one-by-one by slowly pointing to each object as you count. They will begin to count visually by recognizing patterns of groups such as what you might see in dominoes.*

- Count out dishes, silverware, and food.
- Sort objects and toys that are alike and different and then count the different groups.
- Count the family members and then set the table by matching the plates, silverware, and glasses one-to-one for each person.
- Count common objects in the playroom, such as crayons, cars, blocks, and balls.
- Count skips and jumps.
- Count the number of times a ball is bounced.

Measurements *are easy to introduce everyday life. A special place in the home where children are measured as they grow taller helps them see an important component of development.*

- Cook together using measuring cups and spoons.
- Use the family scales to weigh daily or weekly and record results.
- Have a special spot for measuring growth.
- Compare different rulers, yard sticks, and other measuring instruments.
- Compare heights of different family members.

Telling time *is easily taught through the routine of daily events, such as when meals are served, when school begins and ends, and when it is time to go to bed.*

- Point out the time on the clock when it is time for different daily routines.
- Talk about the times designated for daily events, such as going to school, after-school pick-up, breakfast, lunch, and dinner.
- Compare digital and analog clocks (clocks with second, minute, and hour hands).

Shape *awareness can be taught first with toy shapes observed throughout the environment.*

- Identify tables shapes such as round, square, or rectangle.
- Talk about the shapes of blocks.
- Name the shape of an object in the room.

Money *can be taught as children can pay for something they want.*

- Allow the child to purchase a cookie at the bakery is a simple experience in learning about spending money.
- Set up a toy store with play money and products to sell.
- Label the cost of the products.

Fractions *can be taught with toys and food.*

- Share fruit by cutting it into parts.
- Use an apple cutter to divide an apple.
- Oranges automatically come in slices. Count the slices in the orange.
- Order a pizza and talk about how many pieces are in the whole pizza.

- Cut and discuss how a whole sandwich can be cut into smaller pieces such as halves or quarters, to make two and four pieces.
- Talk about a dozen eggs and half a dozen.
- Have the child pay for a small toy at the store then talk about the change.

Temperature *can be taught by measuring, charting, and observing.*

- Hang a thermometer outside to check the daily temperature.
- Chart the weather over time.
- Temperature can be taught during daily routines, by asking the questions such as, "Can you go outside and let me know if you need a coat? If it is snowing, what should you wear?"
- Draw pictures of seasonal changes.

Opportunities arise daily to use numbers and math concepts. Opportunities to apply counting, measuring, using money, identifying fractions, naming geometrical shapes, and learning math terms should be promoted and encouraged through meaningful everyday experiences.

The following lists provide a variety of math related activities and ideas to incorporate into learning with children.

Basic Math Term & Concept - Comparisons

- Big - Little
- Long - Short
- High - Low
- Wide - Narrow
- Late - Early
- First, Middle, Last
- Same/Alike - Different

- Inside - Outside
- Together - Apart
- In Front - Behind
- Near - Far
- Thick - Thin
- Over - Under
- Fast - Slow
- Many - Few
- Odd - Even
- Positive - Negative
- Add - Subtract
- Multiply - Divide

Basic Math Topics & Simple Activities

Counting

- **Numerals and numbers** - Use plastic and magnet numbers
- **Rote counting** - Count objects, toys, and food
- **One-to-one correspondence** - Match similar sets of objects one-to-one
- **One-to-one counting** - Count sets of objects by pointing to each
- **Ordinal numbers** - Count shapes and small toys
- **Addition and subtraction** - Use objects, numerals
- **Positive and negative number** - Make a number line

Measurements

- **Height** (foot, inches) - Measure with a yard stick, ruler, or other measuring tool
- **Weight** (ounces, pounds) - Examine different types of scales
- **Dozen** (12) - Use a clean egg carton to count objects

- **Pint, quart, half-gallon, gallon** - Explore different sizes of containers
- **Cup, 1/2, 1/3, 1/4, 1/8, 1/16** - Bake cookies

Time

- **Hours, minutes, seconds** - Use a clock to notice time
- **Clocks, watches** - Explore toy clocks and watches
- **Morning, noon, evening** - Find photos and picture in books

Geometric Shapes

- **Circle, square, rectangle, triangle** - Sort and draw shapes
- **Area, perimeter** - Find areas outside to walk around

Money

- **Change:** pennies, nickels, dimes, quarter - Play store with play or real money
- **Dollar** - Play games with toy money

Fractions

- **1/4, 1/3, 1/2 and whole** - Measure food: pizza, fruit, candy

Temperature

- **Measurement, estimates** - Study the characteristics of an outdoor thermometer.

Math materials and activities need to be hands on so children can learn about the different areas of math. Simply playing with blocks provides opportunity for learning about shapes, space, counting, measurement, and fractions. Children need a variety of materials for exploration. If materials are limited the kitchen is a wonderful place to teach math concepts. Hands-on experiences based on real life situations are basic for children to learn mathematics. They need to be able to explore using a wide variety of objects to learn math concepts.

| 8 |

Technology

Technology has become an integral part and way of life. The cell phone has become an extension of who we are, providing information at the touch of a fingertip. Children are curious about the world around them and eager to learn, and this includes the technology they observe adults using. Children love to talk on the phone to family members. When our children were young, we had a Radio Shack computer hooked up to the television. One of our first computer purchases was a keyboard so they could learn to type and play games. This was one of the early introductions in the home to computer technology.

Today there are many forms of technology available. Children enjoy exploring and using the different types of technology available, such as the television, mobile phones, tablet devices, smart watches, and computers. Children's explorations of technology should initially be done with adult supervision. Many toys have computer base, such as books that read to children. Access to the Internet should be controlled and needs to be monitored.

The National Association for the Education of Young Children recommends how to use technology tools and interactive media (NAEYC website, 2021).

- Allow children to freely explore touch screens loaded with a wide variety of developmentally appropriate interactive media experiences that are well designed and enhance feelings of success.
- Provide opportunities for children to begin to explore and feel comfortable using "traditional" mouse and keyboard computers to use websites or look up answers with a search engine.
- Capture photos of block buildings or artwork that children have created; videotape dramatic play to replay for children.
- Celebrate children's accomplishments with digital media displayed on a digital projector or on a classroom website.

Mathematics, science and technology activities can be designed and created within the home to help children learn to think and solve problems. Math includes a wide range of basic knowledge children need to learn before starting to school. Simply counting in the car while driving can be a learning experience. Science and awareness of surroundings using simple nature walks can be a fascinating time for family members. Technology can introduce to the children to a wide range of information. Simply watching informational videos provide knowledge for children. Parents and teachers following up and building on experiences enhances learning

- Incorporate assistive technologies as appropriate for children with special needs and/or developmental delays.
- Record children's stories about their drawings or play; make digital audio or video files to document their progress.
- Explore digital storytelling with children. Co-create digital books with photos of the children's play, experiences, or work; attach digital audio files with the child as the narrator.

Preschool children are fascinated by the games on electronic gadgets. These games are good for young children's hand and eye coordination, but they are addictive and need to have time limits. Children enjoy simple games which can also be educational, and they are a good way to have children begin to explore technology and interactive media. Parent-approved movies and games can be loaded onto devices for children to use. Children's movies are abundant and can be downloaded but should contain minimum violence.

Technology has become an important way of life in our society and children enjoy exploring and learning through interactive media. These tools should be used appropriately and intentionally within limits that provide safety for children. Parents and teachers need to set limits on children's ability to explore independently, especially on the computer, so that information and resources are used with the appropriate intentions. It is essential that adults set limits, use tools to control the types of sites that can be accessed, and make sure there is close supervision. Children should be taught the rules and limits for using electronics that the adults responsible establish. It is important to set the devices so the contacts can be controlled, and viewing can be tracked.

In 2020, due to COVID, online school experiences created a new reality in how children learn and are educated. These changes have created challenges for students, educators, and parents. Perhaps it will create an atmosphere in the community that gives everyone involved more respect for their different roles. Parents need support in guiding and monitoring their children's schoolwork. Technology provided the tools to continue education during the COVID crisis.

Children's movies are abundant and can be downloaded for young children's enjoyment. Movies with minimum violence should be a priority. It is important to discuss violence on television and games so children will know they are not real. They see actors being killed and tomorrow they are alive in another movie. Knowing and understanding real and acting must be an important priority during these early years.

Set rules and limits for using electronics. It is important to set the electronics so the contacts can be controlled, and the viewing can be tracked. Family time together is important, and time should be set

ACTIVITIES & IDEAS TO ENRICH YOUNG CHILDREN'S LANGUAGE - 59

aside for family, friends, and teachers without electronics. Electronics should not become the babysitter. They need to be controlled and monitored.

As children grow up in this digital age, parents play an important role in providing, supporting and teaching technology skills. The American Academy of Pediatrics recommends the following major issues when using digital media. Some of their basic suggestions are:

- Make a family media plan together. This plan should fit the family structure, values and parenting style. This plan should be structured to meet the unique activities of the family such as "face to face interaction, family-time, outdoor-play, exercise, unplugged downtime, and sleep". An example might be to have a night the family plays games together each week.
- Monitor media use. Set limits and controls for media use. Be familiar with the applications, platforms, and websites used online. For preschool children put applications on the device to initially control the usage. As children get older, it is important to discuss pitfalls and danger of using social media. Discuss the importance of controlling the content of personal media and what should be kept out of media. Control media through passwords.
- Maintain a balance of play, media, and other activities. Plan activities for the family and child together and monitor activities to ensure balance. Review the family's week to determine how much time is spent using technology.
- Screen time should not always be alone time. Select games and activities that encourage co-engagement. As children grow older, they will play electronic games with friends. These games and activities need to be monitored.
- Be a good role model. As an adult, model the use of good manners online. Take time to interact with the child and encourage them

to share their experiences. For example, all electronics must be turned off during family meals.
- Know the value of face-to-face communication. "Very young children learn best through two-way communication. Engaging in back-and-forth "talk time" is critical for language development." Video chats can be done with extended family members. Grandparents enjoy talking to children on Facetime or other avenues of communication.
- Create tech-free zones. Keep family mealtimes, other family and social gatherings, and children's bedrooms screen free. Set times and places for using digital devices. Be sure to follow-through with the rules for using technology.
- Do not use technology as an emotional pacifier. Encourage children to be independent when playing and interacting within the environment and avoid using media to keep children calm and quiet. Encourage playtime with friends that excludes technology to maintain a balance to avoid overuse of technology.
- Remember: Kids will be kids. Use teachable moments. Continue to monitor and discuss the safety and dangers of using media. Have a regular check-in time for media usage when children are old enough to use the Internet (https://www.healthychildren.org/English/family-life/Media/Pages/Tips-for-Parents-Digital-Age.aspx). As a parent it is important to monitor media for the safety of the child.

Basic technology tools and simple activities

Television
- Select children's educational programs.
- Select children's cartoons and movies.

Mobile Phone
- Encourage conversations with family members.
- Use the timer.

Electronic Toys
- Select electronic toys that each literacy skills such as visual matching, identification, and naming.
- Provide electronics that read books to young children.
- Select electronic games that focus on basic concepts such as shapes, colors, numbers, and letters.

Tablets/iPads
- Download simple fun games.
- Add educational games in math.
- Add early childhood books.
- Download favorite children's movies.
- Research information with young children and read the information.
- Explore activities to do in the community with the child.
- Use the tablet/iPad as a dictionary for spelling words.

Laptops/Computers
- Encourage children to dictate experiences.
- Create books from children's experiences.
- Research information.

Electronic Games
- Select games that promote fine and large motor skills.
- Provide games focused on education.
- Select age-appropriate electronic game

Today media is an important component of daily life. Controlling the type of media is important for preschool children and as children mature. After developing a family plan follow-through on how media will be used so children know the rules and monitor time spent. Children can experience educational games, view age-appropriate movies, and communicate with a controlled message application. Set up regular check-in times, and model appropriate use of tools.

The preschool years are a time of high motivation for learning. Children enjoy exploring the world around them. During this time, they can learn basic skills and concepts in science, math, and technology that will prepare them for school success. Through quality activities and a well-planned environment, children can explore, discover, and experiment in interactive ways through play and face-to-face interaction to learn basic skills and concepts appropriate to their developmental age.

PART IV - CREATIVE ARTS

Young children should be given sufficient opportunities to express themselves through the creative arts. Exploration through art, music and drama provides ways in which children can communicate and express feelings. Setting up a place in the home or in the early childhood classroom for creative arts activities will encourage creative expression. All types of activities can be a part of daily experiences.

The creative arts included in this section are:

- *Art*
- *Music*
- *Drama*

Creative arts are a valuable avenue for expression and communication. In the early years, children need to frequently be able to communicate who they are through scribbling and drawing. They need opportunities to sing children's classical songs and express themselves through music. Real-life situations and appropriate fantasy stories can both be dramatized. Characters in books, videos, movies, and television media designed especially for children can be imitated.

| 9 |

Art

Young children love to observe and experiment. They learn about art and artistic expression by using materials that allow them to draw, color, model with clay, and work with materials for cutting and gluing. The kitchen table is a good place to provide art materials where their use can be easily supervised by an adult. Painting works best in a closely supervised area. Open-ended activities can provide an outlet for expression that can be satisfying and relaxing (Castle, 1966).

Common art design elements including line, color, shape, form, value, space, texture, unity/harmony and point can provide prompts for talking about a child's art. Color, shape, and texture can be discussed. In the home or preschool, children can easily learn about color, shape, and texture by talking about the characteristics of the object. Preschool children should learn to recognize colors, name them, and begin to read some color words. Adult verbal interaction is essential for teaching color names as children first imitate color names, then move to identifying the color in artworks, naming colors, and reading the color word.

One step-by-step process adapted from Montessori for teaching colors and many other new ideas is:

1. Adults point to and names the color.
2. The child is asked to find the color from among a group of objects or pictures of different colors.
3. The child names the color of an object.
4. The child learns to read the word associated with color.

Children need to be able to explore the use of colors when drawing representations. Young children begin with scribbles, progress to naming their scribbled drawings, then move to creating more recognizable forms. Rhonda Kellogg (1979) studied early patterns in how children learn to draw. Early scribbles are followed by progression to a pre-schematic stage during the preschool years. Children begin experiencing art by scribbling. During this period of artistic development, children primarily repeat interesting and varied lines and circles as they move from simple scribbles to naming and connecting their scribbles to real-world objects.

Learning how to sculpt with clay

One activity that can best enrich the artistic experience for children is to label their scribbles. A child will name their scribbles and later their artwork will begin to form a better representation of the world as they grow into the pre-schematic stage.

As children struggle, sometimes they feel helpless when trying to create forms. The parent or other present adult can discuss basic shapes such as circles, rectangles, triangles, and squares. These basic shapes can be used to draw representations. For example, a circle can be a head. Circles, triangles, and rectangles can represent the body parts. Adults can talk about these shapes and show children how to create what they see using shapes.

Art topics and suggested activities

- **Drawing** - Provide plain paper and pencils
- **Coloring** - Create a box with colored crayons, pencils and markers.
- **Cutting** - Make children's scissors available for exploration.
- **Gluing** - Glue sticks are easy for young children to use.
- **Craft materials** - Provide seeds, yarn, fabric swatches, buttons, pom-pom balls, and other safe objects.
- **Painting** - Provide a small watercolor set.
- **Playdough** - Make homemade playdough recipes found on the Internet.

Simple art materials can be set up in a special space in the home and are a must in an early childhood classroom.

- Children enjoy coloring, cutting, gluing, and creating.
- Children need to be taught how to hold and use pencils, crayons, and scissors correctly by observing adult models who show them how they are used.
- Pencils and crayons should be held between the thumb and pointer finger balanced on the middle finger, with the ring finger and little finger curled under the pencil or crayon for balance.
- Scissors should be blunt and safe for use during the early years.
- Plastic scissors designed to be used with either the left- or right-hand work well.
- How to hold scissors needs to be modeled and taught.
- Safe, appropriate use of scissors is an especially important discussion to have so that children will avoid accidents.
- Talk about, such things as not cutting hair because this can be another exploration of using scissors that children may do.

> A basic art activity is gluing objects with interesting textures such as yarn, scrap fabrics, buttons, and small pom-pom balls onto paper or cardboard. Seed and dry beans and macaroni also make interesting textures for art. Different scraps around the house can be used. This type of activity gives an opportunity to discuss design and balance.

Although coloring books are a component of our culture, they have historically been viewed as a media that limits creativity. More recently, they have been used as a form of relaxation. Plain paper can provide an opportunity for children to express themselves in a more open-ended way. Instead of using a coloring book, reading a story or taking a walk to explore nature before creating original art can provide inspiration for a more original art expression. Reading a version of classics like *The Three Bears* and then talking about it can provide a good prompt to encourage children's art creation. Talking about how many circles need to be used to create each of the three bears can give children the confidence to draw, since bears can be drawn with multiple circles.

> Visiting an art museum can be a rich experience for children to learn about the different art mediums such as oils, collages, watercolor, sculptures, and photography. They can learn about texture, colors, shapes, and other elements used for expressing feelings and representations of the environment.

One way to build children's confidence is by directly instructing them in how to draw using basic shapes. An oval can be a body, a circle a head, parallel sticks and rectangles can be arms, legs, fingers, and a neck. Stick lines can be fingers, circles can be eyes, swirly lines can be curly hair, a crescent shape can be a mouth, eyebrows, parts of the nose, and ears. Once children learn to use basic shapes to create people, animals, and other things, they can enjoy art without feeling helpless or frustrated.

Children's books provide another way to expose children to art. The classic artwork in such artist as Eric Carle, Jr. children's books provide limitless examples of how to use color and texture with bold cutouts to represent common objects and things. Caldecott award winning children's books are known for their art media and will provide ideas for different art media to use with young children.

Provide a special place in the home for children to express themselves through art. Initially, this should be a supervised area as children learn how to use and care for art materials. Once they learn, they can use the materials unsupervised. Begin with basic art activities. Providing rich art experiences can promote not only creative expression, but also learning about the world and practice with important fine motor skills.

| 10 |

Music

A love for music can begin even before birth as the expecting mother plays or listens to classical music. There are books and programs for parents that focus on music before and after birth. Once children are born, playing soothing music can help develop an appreciation for listening and in addition to promoting relaxation.

Families who enjoy music and sing together provide models for their children. The research study led by Benjamin Bloom (1985) emphasized the importance of building talent areas. Bloom's study documents patterns of parenting that led to the development of the expertise of well-known musicians, athletes, scientists, and mathematicians. Parents who possessed a high interest in the area and engaged a coach or teacher for their child provided the framework for the development of expertise.

During the early childhood years there are activities that can be done with music. Encourage activities such as singing, listening and moving to music, playing instruments, and dramatizing stories about music. Below is a list of some of ideas.

Music experiences and activities

- **Listening to music** - Listen to different types of music.

- **Singing to music** - Sing favorite children's songs.
- **Moving/Dancing to music** - Provide old scarfs to wave along with the music.
- **Playing simple instruments** - Play rhythm band instruments and musical toys.
- **Dramatizing with music** - Dramatize excerpts from movies.

Listening to different types of music can be a good auditory experience. Children can learn the different sounds and vocabulary such as high, low, slow, and fast to describe music. They need opportunities to hear different types of music and listen to a variety of music genre, such as classical and popular.

Children need opportunities to sing along to music. Riding in the car is a perfect time to listen and sing along to music. **Singing** old classic early childhood songs can begin with CDs played in the car or at home. A favorite collection of classic early childhood songs CDs first published in 1980 and continually revised can be found in the *Wee Sing and Play* series by Pamela Conn Beall and Susan Hagen Nipp. The songs in this series are classic songs that children have enjoyed for generations. There are a variety of categories focusing on topics such as silly songs, nursery rhymes, campfire favorites, and finger plays. *The Wee Sing and Play* series can be found on websites, in local bookstores, and on YouTube. Other resources focusing on music for children can be found by exploring websites, bookstores, and music stores.

Another fun activity that children love is **moving to music**. Moving to music provides children an opportunity to listen and experience rhythms. Children can be provided with scarves and encouraged to move with them as they listen to music. Scarves will provide an escape from thinking so much about self and instead direct the children's concentration to the movement and flow of the fabric while they listen and move to the music. Dance steps and body movement can also be taught.

Learning to play a traditional Korean hand drum called a Solo

Children love to **play musical instruments**. Beginning rhythm instruments like drums, sticks, bells, and tambourines are just a few that children can play. Formal music lessons provide opportunities for children to play other instruments like the violin, piano, or guitar as they are developmentally ready. Children can be taught simple tunes to play on a piano rather than just banging on the keys. We found old Rhythm Band sticks at an antique store and they stimulated dramatic exploration and performance for the family. Adults with experience in playing the piano, guitar, and violin can teach basics before more formal instruction.

Dramatizing musicals can be fun. Listening to music that inspires emotion using a variety of sounds can encourage children to express feelings. Old classical music based on a story set to music, such as "Peter and the Wolf" by Sergei Prokofiev and "The Nutcracker" by Tchaikovsky, can be dramatized. Adults can work together with children to make costumes to dramatize the story to music. Children can make puppets of the characters and act out the musical story. The wonderful children's folk literature and variations that have been made into songs and movies, such as Disney's *Frozen*, cannot be overlooked.

All facets of music, singing, listening, playing instruments, movement, and dramatization provide an important learning experience for young children. They can learn to appreciate and distinguish sounds, melodies, and rhythms, and connect stories, and movement to music. Music lifts the spirits and is fun for both adults and children.

| 11 |

Drama

Drama evolves out of movement, expression, and stories. Children can begin simply by dramatizing folk tales such as "The Three Bears," "Three Billy Goats Gruff," and "The Three Little Pigs." Today, children's movies provide exciting prompts for learning and character study with stories that have incredible settings, costumes, and music. Many children love wearing costumes that represent characters in movies. Costumes of favorite characters are easily found online or at children's toy stores or they can be made by the children. Children will be able to explore different movements and actions by dramatizing familiar stories, including those adapted to movies.

Basic drama activities and ideas

- **Large locomotor movements** - Encourage running, jumping, skipping, walking, hopping, etc.
- **Creative movement** - Express feelings through movement
- **Dress-up props** - Dramatize excerpts from movies and stories
- **Simple props** - Pretend conversation with old telephone
- **Colorful props** - Move using colored scarves
- **Puppet theater** - Tell stories with puppets

- **Dramatize special experiences** - Role play going camping
- **Dramatize daily experiences in the home and going to a store** - Provide props such as old clothing, dishes, toy food, toy cash register, etc.

Drama can also be used to teach children basic scripts for discussing social skills and traveling. Scripts can be simple and open ended, so children learn what to do in a variety of situations. Also, experience simple activities such as going to a special event. Before going to a special event, or dinner out at either a fast-food place or upscale restaurant, role play to help children plan what to say, how to act, and what might be needed for each situation.

> When I taught kindergarten, children loved to pretend going camping. They would do elaborate preparations of selecting materials and planning for the trip. Children can study maps and brochures of different state and national parks.

Let the child help prepare for the outing, if appropriate to the occasion, they might prepare a snack, get coats ready, or gather other items that will be needed for the event.

Role play ideas

- **Family members** - Father, mother, brother, sister, baby, grandfather, grandmother, aunts, uncles, and others
- **Community helpers** - Mail person, Police person, Fire person, Doctor, Nurse, Zookeeper, Plumber, Bus driver, Grocery store employee, Pilot, Taxi driver, and others
- **Folk tale or movie characters** - The Three Bears, Three Billy Goats, Beauty and the Beast, Frozen, Mulan, and many others

- **Superheroes** - Batman, Robin, Wonder Woman, Black Panther, Ironman, Captain Marvel, and others
- **Holidays and common events** - Thanksgiving, camping trips, and others

Today there are miniature sets for role playing and imitating interesting characters and events. Children have access to a treasure of folk tales and new stories in books, cartoons, and live-action movies. Dramatization can be used to teach story sequence. Over the past few decades, Disney and other studios have created wonderful movies accompanied by music that enriches the storytelling. Who can forget the beautiful song, "Let It Go," in Disney's movie *Frozen!*

Adults can help children build sets, write plays, create costumes, and dramatize old and new stories. The book, *Birds Being Birds* by this author can be dramatized and sung, with the movements in the story encouraging basic locomotor skills for young children.

Drama can motivate creative thinking as adults and children work to create fantasy and real-life experiences in make-believe settings. Favorite books can come alive. Homes and classrooms can be transformed by using props and costumes. Telling stories through drama is captivating.

Creative arts provide an outlet for expression and pretending for children to explore different behaviors through music, art, and drama. Setting up places in the home or classroom for children to explore the arts can be diverse and responsive to children and family interests. Simple activities such as listening quietly to music, drawing, and videos of movies can provide time for thinking and expressing. Children can learn new songs, create costumes and props, and dramatize movies. The range of activities are broad and can be done quietly or enthusiastically together.

SUMMARY

The ideas and activities presented are based on practices that have proven effective in the education of children when used by parents and early childhood educators. As adults begin to think of the young child's world as a place for inquiry through exploration, discovery, and invention of ideas, a new world is opened and creates freedom to expand children's knowledge in exciting and motivating ways. **The recommended activities and ideas will enrich each young child's environment inside and outside the home or early childhood classroom.** Young children are eager learners and need a wide range of experiences to be prepared for the educational expectations of today. As parents expand their role from caregiver to teacher, it is important to remember that children need well rounded experiences that reflect the world around them. Children are encouraged to expand their knowledge and learn through enrichment activities that take them beyond the everyday world.

Literacy and language development are the primary focus of the first section and integrated throughout other sections to promote all types of learning by building an academic vocabulary. The foundation of the ideas and activities is to build a firm foundation with an experiential knowledge-base grounded in oral and written language.

Today there is a renewed interest in children's social and emotional development. As families and educators spend more time focused on technology, it is even more important that children need to be guided and encouraged in how to relate to others. They need to learn that rules and behavioral expectations vary in different environments and need consistent guidance and direction so that they can be successful and take pride in their choices and actions. Knowing individual family expectation and rules in multiple situations and how to adapt is essential to successful interactions.

Learning academic skills in math and science before formal education begins, prepares children be ready for the classroom. In addition, the use of technology today is a way of life in society and maintaining a balance with children is extremely important for them to develop oral language and communication skills with others. Those children who have access to technology during the preschool years have important resources for learning than those without.

The creativity component of learning is essential and can be captured within the creative arts to provide an outlet for creative and thinking expression. Children's practical learning experiences need to be balanced with opportunities to express themselves creatively.

Adults play an important role in guiding the children's development by building strong relationships. The DOING of enrichment experiences together as a family and classroom can build a foundation of confidence as children relate and learn from the caring adults. Building the groundwork for young children's ability to respond to a complex society full of knowledge and information is essential. Our country needs a strong society where children can filter information that is accurate and understood to be confident contributing citizens.

RESOURCES & REFERENCES

Bailey, Alison L. and Margaret Heritage. Formative Assessment for Literacy Grades K-12. Thousand Oaks, CA: Corwin Press, 2008.

Baines, Lawrence. A Teacher's Guide to Multisensory Learning – Improving Literacy by Engaging the Senses. Alexandria, Virginia: Association for Supervision and Curriculum Development, 2008.

Bamberger, Honi and Patricia Huges. Super Graphs, Venns, and Glyphs. New York: Scholastic Professional Books, 1995.

Beall, Pamela Conn and Susan Hagen Nipp. Wee Sing Around the Campfire. Los Angeles, Price Stern Sloan Publisher Inc., 1980.

Beall, Pamela Conn and Susan Hagen Nipp. Wee Sing Children's Songs and Fingerplays. Los Angeles, Price Stern Sloan Publisher Inc., 1980.

Beall, Pamela Conn and Susan Hagen Nipp. Wee Sing Musical Games and Rhymes for Children, Price Stern Sloan Publisher Inc., 1980.

Beall, Pamela Conn and Susan Hagen Nipp. Wee Sing Silly Songs. Los Angeles, Price Stern Sloan Publisher Inc., 1980.

Bloom, Benjamin, ed. Developing Talent in Young People. New York: Ballantine Books, 1985.

Brown, Margaret Wise. Ill by Clement Hurd. Good Night Moon. Harper, 1947.

Burns, M. Susan, Peg Griffin and Catherine E. Snow, ed. Starting Out Right. Washington, DC: National Academy Press, 1999.

Carle, Eric, The Very Hungry Caterpillar. New York, NY: Scholastic Publishing, 1977.

Carter, Carolyn J. "Why Reciprocal Teaching?" Educational Leadership. Association for Supervision and Curriculum Development. pp. 64-68, Vol. 54, No.6, March, 1997.

Castle, A.D. and Para Porter. Practical Ideas and Activities for Pre-School Enrichment Programs. Wolfe City, Texas: Henington Publishing Company,1966.

Cecil, Nancy. Striking a Balance – Positive Practices for Early Literacy. Scottsdale, Arizona: Holcomb Hathaway, Pub., 1999.

Clay, Marie M. An Observation Survey. Auckland, New Zealand: Heinemann Educational Books, Inc. 1993.

Clay, Marie M. Becoming Literate. Portsmouth, N.H.: Heinemann Educational Books, Inc., 1991.

Clay, Marie M. Reading Recovery, A Guidebook for Teachers in Training. Portsmouth, N.H.: Hinemann Educational Books, Inc., 1993.

Collins, Ray. Reading Helpers: A Handbook for Training Tutors. Washington, DC: The Corporation for National Service Training and Technical Assistance Unit and Vienna, VA: The Early Childhood Technical Assistance Center, 1998.

Clayton R. Cook, Kirk R. Williams, Nancy G. Guerra, Tia E. Kim, and Shelly Sadek. Predictors of Bullying and Victimization in Childhood and Adolescence: A Meta-analytic Investigation. American Psychological Association, 1045-3830/10, DOI: 10.1037/a0020149, 2010.

Cox, Joshua, Brandon Foster, David Bamat. A review of instruments for measuring social and emotional learning skills among secondary students. United States Department of Education, Institute of Educational Sciences, and National Center for Education Evaluation and Regional Assistance, 2019.

Cunningham, Patricia and Richard Allington. Classrooms that Work They Can All Read and Write. Boston: Pearson Allyn and Bacon, 2007.

Dorn, Linda J., Cathy French, and Tammy Jones. Apprenticeship in Literacy. York, Maine: Steinhouse Pub., 1998.

Durkin, Deloris. Getting Reading Started. Boston, Massachusetts: Allyn and Bacon, 1982.

Education Week Research Center. Safety and SEL Survey. Bethesda, MD: Education Week, 2019.

Fountas, Irene and Gay Su Pinnell. Guided Reading. Portsmouth, New Hampshire: Heinemann, 1996.

Frey, Nancy and Douglas Fisher. Rigorous Reading. Thousand Oaks, CA: Corwin Literacy, 2013.

Galdone, Paul. Gingerbread Boy. McGraw-Hill, 1978.

Glazer, Joan. Literature for Young Children. New York: Macmillan Pub. Co., 1991.

Goethel, Jan. ed. By Susan Paull Shane and Ronna Spacone. Frontiers in Family Literacy. Louisville, Ky: National Center for Family Literacy, 1996.

Gunning, Thomas. Best Books for Beginning Readers. Allyn and Bacon, 1998.

Hart, Betty and Todd R. Risley. Meaningful Differences in the Everyday Experiences of Young American Children. Boston: Paul H. Brooks Publisher, 1995.

Hattie, John. Visible Learning A Synthesis of Over 800 Meta-Analyses Relating to Achievement. London: Routledge Taylor & Francis Group: 2008.

Hattie, John. Visible Learning for Teachers Maximizing Impact on Learning. London: Routledge Taylor & Francis Group, 2012.

Hoyt, Linda. Snapshots – Literacy Minilessons Up Close. Portsmouth, New Hampshire: Heinemann, 2000.

Hiebert, E. H. Selecting Texts for Beginning Reading Instruction, CIERA Homepage http://www.ciera.org., 1997.

Holdaway, Don. The Foundations of Literacy. Ashton Scholastic, 1979.

Huck, Charlotte S. and Barbara Z. Kiefer. 8th ed. Children's Literature in the Elementary School. New York: McGraw Hill Company, Inc. 2004.

Hull, Marion A. and Barbara J. Fox. Phonics for the Teaching of Reading. 7th ed. Columbus, Ohio: Merrill an imprint of Prentice Hall, 1994.Jalongo, Mary Kellogg, Rhonda. Children's Drawings/Children's Minds. New York: Avon, 1979.

Renck and Deborah McDonald Ribblett. "Using Song Picture Books to Support Emergent Literacy." Childhood Education. Olney, MD: Association for Childhood Education International, Fall 1997, Vol. 74, No. 1.

Jewell, Margaret and Miles Zintz. Learning to Read Naturally. Kendall/Hunt Pub. Co., 1986.

Katz, l. G. and D.E. McClellan. Fostering Children's Social Competence: The Teacher's Role. Washington DC: National Association for the Education of Young Children, 1997.

Kostelnik, Marjorie J., Alice Phipps Whiren, Anne K. Soderman, Laura C. Stein, Kara Gregory. Guiding Children's 4th ed. Guiding Children's Social Development. Albany, NY: 2002.

Koralek, Derry and Ray Collins. America Reads Challenge – On the Road to Reading A Guide for Community Partners. Washington, DC: The Corporation for National Service Training and Technical Assistance Unit and Vienna, VA: The Early Childhood Technical Assistance Center, 1997.

Kratcoski, Annette and Karyn Bobkoff Katz. "Talking with Children in Teaching Language Learners in the Classroom. Young Children. Washington, D.D.: National Association for the Education of Young Children. Vol. 53, Number 3, May 1998.

Marzano, Robert. Building Background Knowledge for Academic Achievement. Alexandria, VA: Association Supervision and Curriculum Development. 2004

Morrow, Lesley. The Literacy Center. York, Maine: Stenhouse Publishers. 1997

Ministry of Education. Dancing with the Pen: The Learner as a Writer. Wellington, New Zealand: Richard C. Owen Pub. Inc., 1992.

Ministry of Education. Reading in the Junior Class. Wellington, New Zealand: Richard C. Owen Pub. Inc., 1963.

Murphy, Marilyn, Sam Redding, and Janet S. Twyman (ed.). Handbook on Personalized Learning for States, Districts, and Schools. Charlotte, NC: Information Age Publishing, Inc., 2016.

Nash, Madeleine. "Fertile Minds." Child Growth and Development 1998/99. Ed.
Ellen Junn and Chris Boyatzis. Sluice Doc, Connecticut: Dushkin/McGraw Hill, 1998.
Nelsen, Marjorie and Jan Nelsen-Parish. Peak with Books. 3rd Ed. Thousand Oaks, California: Corwin Press, Inc. 1999.
O'Brien-Palmer. Michelle. BOOK TALK exciting literature experiences for kids. Kirkland, WA: MicNik Pub., Inc., 1993.
Opitz, Michael. Getting the Most from Predictable Books. New York: Scholastic Professional Books, 1995.
Orzkus, Lori. Keynote Speaker: "Comprehension and Guided Reading: Best Ever Literacy Survival Tips." Edmond: Oklahoma. Association Supervision and Curriculum Development. November 6, 2014.
Perrault, Charles. Ill. Errol Le Cain. Cinderella. Puffin Books, 1976.
Pinnell, Gay Su and Irene C. Fountas. A Coordinator's Guide to Help America Read. Portsmouth, NH: Heinemann, 1997.
Pinnell, Gay Su and Irene C. Fountas. Word Matters. Portmouth, NH: Heinemann. 1998.
Piper, Walter. The Little Engine that Could. Platt & Munk, Pub, MCMXLV.
Popp, Marcia S. Learning Journals in the K-8 Classroom. Mahwah, NJ: Lawrence Erlbaum Associates, Pub., 1997.
Potter, Jana, Judy Blankenship and Laura Carlsmith. So That Every Child Can Read... America Reads Community Tutoring Partnerships. Portland, Oregon: Northwest Regional Educational Laboratory, 1999.
Richardson, Donna Castle. Birds Being Birds, Edmond, OK: Educational Dynamics, 2nd ed. 2018.
Richardson, Donna Castle. Little Lilly Ladybug, Edmond, OK: Educational Dynamics, 2nd ed. 2018.
Routman, Regie. Invitations. Portsmouth, NH: Heinemann, 1991.
Searfoss, Lyndon W., Thomas W. Bean, and Jeffry I. Gelfer. Developing Literacy Naturally. Dubuque, Iowa: Kendall/Hunt Publishing Co., 1998.

Shore, Rima. Rethinking the Brain: New Insights into Early Development. New York, New York: Families and Work Institute, 1997.

Sousa, David A. 2nd.ed. How the Brain Learns to Read Thousand Oaks, California: Corwin A Sage Company. 2014.

Snow, Kyle. Bullying in Early Childhood, National Association for the Education of Young Children. Website Resource, 2014.

Taylor, Denny. Family Literacy. London: Heinemann Educational Books, 1983.

Thompkins, Gail E. Language Arts Patterns of Practices. Columbus Ohio: Pearson, 2005.

Thompkins, Gail E. Literacy for the 21st Century. 6th ed. Upper Saddle River, New Jersey: Pearson, 2013.

Tompkins, Gail E., Teaching Writing. Columbus, Ohio, 1990.

Trelease, Jim. The Read Aloud Handbook. New York: Penguin Books, 1987.

Vaugh, Sharon and Sylvia Linan-Thompson. Research-Based Methods of Reading Instruction Grades K-3. Alexandria, Virginia: Association for Supervision and Curriculum Development, 2004.

Wells, Gordon. The Meaning Makers. Portsmouth, New Hampshire: Heinemann, 1986.

Woods, Audrey. The Napping House. Ill. Don Wood. SanDiego: Harcourt Brace Jovanich, Pub., 1984.

Wolfe, Pat and Ron Brandt. "What Do We Know from Brain Research?" Educational Leadership. Effingham, Illinois: Association for supervision and Curriculum and Instruction, Vol. 56, No. 3, November 1998.

Yopp, Hallie and Ruth Helen Yopp. Literature-Based Reading Activities. 2nd ed. Boston, Massachusetts: Allyn and Bacon, 1996.

https://aisdsel.files.wordpress.com/2015/01/sel-competencies-wheel.png - Research on social competencies that can be reviewed and examined to support the social development and overall well-being of the child.

https://casel.org/ - Website has information on social and emotional learning based on research, accepted practice, and polices for leaders and educators focused on the advancement of social and emotional learning for all students.

http://csefel.vanderbilt.edu/familytools/teaching_emotions.pdf - Great suggestions for teaching children how to identify and express emotions in an acceptable manner.

https://charactercounts.org/program-overview/ - Character Counts located at Drake University highlights Six Pillars of Character are: Trustworthiness, Respect, Responsibility, Fairness, Caring and Citizenship. We recommend always using the Pillars in this specific order and using the acronym "T.R.R.F.C.C." (terrific).

http://www.edcentral.org/vocabulary - Loewenberg, Aaron. "New Research: Two-Year-Old Vocabulary Predicts Kindergarten Success". September 23, 2015.

https://www.healthychildren.org/English/family-life/Media/Pages/Tips-for-Parents-Digital-Age.aspx - Media and digital devices are an integral part of our world today. The importance of face-to-face time with family, friends, and teachers plays a pivotal and important role in promoting children's learning and healthy development.

http://www.playideas.com/25-bubble-activities-preschoolers/ - A wide variety of bubble activities suggested for preschooler. The body bubble is a great addition to the literature. Colors used in water should be washable.

https://www.healthychildren.org/English/family-life/Media/Pages/Tips-for-Parents-Digital-Age.aspx - Recommendations for planning and using digital media with young children.

http://my.ilstu.edu/~eostewa/ART309/Five_Stages.htm - Explains the historical developmental stage of art to include: scribbling, preschematic, schematic, transitional, realism. Preschool children's artistic development can be seen in the scribbling (Salome R. A. and Moore, B. E., 2015).

https: https://www.naeyc.org/resources/blog/bullying-early-childhood - Article discusses an overview of bullying and the importance of learning social skills and self-regulation.

//www.naeyc.org/resources/topics/technology-and-media/preschoolers-and-kindergartners - Recommends research-based ways for young children to use the computer through exploration.

http://onlinelibrary.wiley.com/doi/10.1111/cdev.12398/full - "Even after extensive covariate adjustment, 24-month-old children with larger oral vocabularies displayed greater reading and mathematics achievement, increased behavioral self-regulation, and fewer externalizing and internalizing problem behaviors at kindergarten entry."

https://rhodakellogg.com/ - Rhoda Kellogg (website, 2019) classic extensive study of young children's art development is outlined through five states to include scribbling, pre-schematic, schematic, transitional, and realism from 1948 to 1981.

https://www.scholastic.com/teachers/articles/teaching-content/learning-be-best-we-can-be/ - Ethel Titthich discusses Building Character in Early childhood Settings. She elaborates on politeness, sharing, honesty, and prosocial behavior.

https://www.socialthinking.com/Articles?name=social-emotional-self-regulation - Adults play an important role in helping children develop by promoting self-awareness, self-regulation, and problem solving. Adults become the teacher by modeling and communicating how to act and what is expected in different situations.

https://theconversation.com/dinntime-storytelling-makes-kids-voracious-readers-47318/ - "Years of research from the Home-School Study of Language and Literacy Development have shown that dinner conversation is a terrific vocabulary booster for young children – even better than reading aloud to them."

http://ucanr.edu/edu/sites/ReadytoSucceed/TypesofBooks/ - "A brief discussion of various genre and types of books that should be offered to young children."

http://www.earlychildhoodnews.com/earlychildhood/article_view.aspx?ArticleId=409%20 - Website has basic ideas for helping children think scientifically. It has a comparison of traditional and new approaches to thinking about science.

https://funlearningforkids.com/science-activities-preschoolers/ - Website has incredible activities for preschoolers. It includes basic experiments that promote scientific thinking.

https://proudtobeprimary.com/social-emotional-activities-distance-learning-at-home/ - Casal recommends five essential areas for academic and relationship success. "They are self-awareness, self-management, social awareness, relationship skills, and responsible decision-making." Suggested children's books for reading about emotions and activities for teaching and clarifying social and emotional behaviors.

https://timtopham.com/how-to-build-an-early-childhood-music-program-from-scratch/ - Website recommends movement activities for young children.

Donna Castle Richardson, Ed.D. serves as the CEO of Educational Dynamics, LLC. She previously served as the Director of the Central Comprehensive Center, one of 15 Comprehensive Centers providing technical assistance with funding from the United States Department of Education through the University of Oklahoma. She also served as the Director of EDUTAS. She is a Professor Emeritus in the Department of Education at Oklahoma City University (OCU) where she designed and directed the teacher certification programs in Early Childhood and Elementary Education teaching early childhood education, curriculum, children's literature, emergent literacy, and reading development.

Dr. Richardson's interest in family literacy research, early reading, children's literature, and school improvement led to national recognition. She evaluated the Oklahoma City Public Schools' Even Start project in which her research and the project design were validated by the U.S. Department of Education's National Diffusion Network and was awarded a National Dissemination Grant. Her Reading Discovery Tutor Training program was featured in the U.S. Department of Education's best practices document *So That Every Child Can Read...America Reads Community and Tutoring Projects.*

This is the fifth book in the Reading with Children Series designed for parents of young children based on best practices to help children be school ready. The use of the enrichment activities and ideas will give young children a head start during the preschool and early years of education.

Donna is married to Don Ray Richardson. Their home is in Edmond, Oklahoma. They have two children and five grandchildren who live in Denver, Colorado.

www.ingramcontent.com/pod-product-compliance
Lightning Source LLC
Chambersburg PA
CBHW041504010526
44118CB00001B/12